14.95

983
Hin
Hintz, Martin
Chile

$14.95

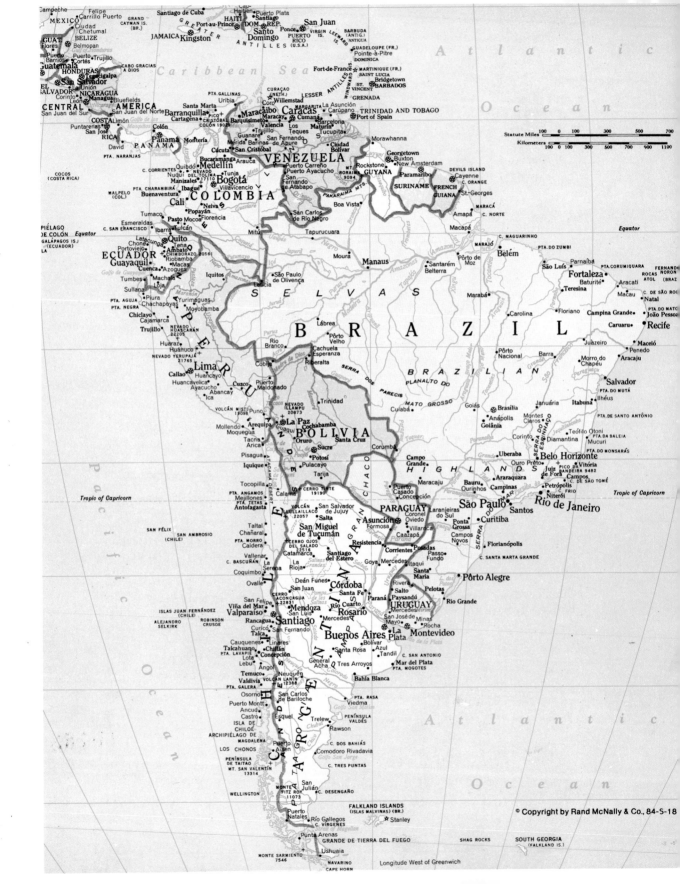

Enchantment of the World

CHILE

By Martin Hintz

Consultant: George I. Blanksten, Professor, Department of Political Science, Northwestern University

Consultant for Chile: Isabel Grau, former Assistant Professor of Latin American History at the University of Chile and researcher for Latin American Center of Demography of the United Nations

Consultant for Reading: Robert L. Hillerich, Ph.D., Bowling Green State University, Bowling Green, Ohio

CHILDRENS PRESS ™

CHICAGO

Lago Puyehue and surrounding farmland beneath Volcán Puyehue, west of Osorno

Chile is dedicated to the people of Chile who have molded a modern nation out of a diverse ethnic and cultural background.

Excerpts from poems and essays by Gabriela Mistral, Pablo Neruda, and Vicente Huidobro, found in Chapter 7, were taken from *The Chilean Cultural Panorama No. 4: Mistral, Neruda, Huidobro— Three Figures in Chilean Literature* (1979, Cultural Department, Embassy of Chile).

Library of Congress Cataloging in Publication Data

Hintz, Martin.
　Chile.

　(Enchantment of the world)
　Includes index.
　Summary: Describes the landscape, history, economy, culture, and people of this extraordinarily long, narrow country.
　1. Chile—Juvenile literature. [1. Chile]
I. Title.
F3058.5.H56　1985　　983　　84-23104
ISBN 0-516-02755-7　　　AACR2

Picture Acknowledgments
©**Victor Englebert**—6, 9 (right), 57 (left), 72, 77 (left)
©**Chandler Forman**—10
Gartman Agency/Photri:
　14 (bottom), 24 (top), 66 (right), 104, 105
　©**Jack Novak**—5, 86
©**Virginia Grimes**—Cover, 50

Hillstrom Stock Photo:
　©**Stacy O'Son**—61 (bottom left), 65 (right), 84 (bottom left)
Martin Hintz—49, 53 (right), 55 (bottom right), 61 (bottom right), 101
Historical Pictures Service, Chicago—29 (left), 30 (2 photos), 33, 37, 39, 45 (left), 87
Image Finders:
　©**Bob Skelly**—16 (left), 58, 63 (right)
　©**Eric Leaper**—63 (left), 96 (top)
　©**Emilie Lepthien**—18 (bottom 2 photos), 27 (right), 35, 55 (bottom left), 56 (bottom), 61 (top), 66 (left), 96 (bottom)
Nawrocki Stock Photo:
　©**Wm. S. Nawrocki**—42
　©**Mark Gamba**—14 (top), 16 (right), 21 (right), 60, 74, 95
　©**Carlos Vergara**—57 (right), 82 (right), 84 (top right), 107 (left and center), 122 (bottom)
Chip and Rosa Peterson—4, 11, 12 (2 photos), 13, 17, 21 (left), 26, 29 (right), 32, 62 (left), 68 (2 photos), 71, 75, 76, 77 (right), 81, 91, 94, 99, 103 (left)
Root Resources—73
　©**Jane Downton**—122 (top)
　©**Grace Lanctot**—80, 92
Roloc Color Slides—24 (bottom), 28 (2 photos), 41, 52, 82 (left)
Stock Imagery/Hillstrom Stock Photo:
　©**A.P.C.**—107 (right)
　©**Pedro Elster**—8, 27 (left), 53 (left), 55 (top), 59, 65 (left), 93
　©**Fairchild**—62 (right), 64, 84 (top left and bottom right), 103 (right)
　©**Leaper**—22 (2 photos), 56 (top)
　©**Wilke**—106
　©**Leander L. Urmy**—9 (left)
Tom Stack and Associates:
　©**Gary Milburn**—18 (top), 67
UPI—20, 45 (right), 47 (2 photos)
Cover: Santa Lucía Park, Santiago

Southern pass of the Continental Divide, between Chile and Argentina

TABLE OF CONTENTS

Huaso team at a rodeo tries to pin a steer against the wall.

Chapter 1

LAND OF THE HUASO

"Ki, ki, ki, ki! Yip, yip, yip!" Federico spurs his rangy brown mare toward the steer. The animal hooks right with its horn, terror in its red-rimmed eyes. The crowd gasps. Federico is able to swerve the horse just out of reach. Then he slams into the side of the steer. The creature hits the wall of the rodeo ring with a breathtaking thud. It then staggers off, heading for the gate held open by a gray-haired old-timer.

The fans cheer Federico as he gallops back around the dusty, semicircular ring, waving his wide-brimmed straw hat. The local rodeo club is putting on today's roughriding exhibition. This is a good run for Federico; he scores well. "Ah, a real *huaso!*" says Señor Valdivia, the livestock buyer from Santiago. Federico's father smiles broadly at the praise.

A real huaso! A real cowboy—Chilean style!

A Chilean rodeo is very different from one in North America. Federico gains points by pushing the steer into certain marks along the wall with his horse. Federico and his riding partner, Raúl, then try to corner it. The team wins or loses depending on how close they can shove the steer to the target area. The best place to hit a steer is in the rear end, to get four points. The head is worth a fat zero but the front shoulder is a two-pointer, with a stomach hit worth three.

Osorno Volcano

The huasos (pronounced "wassos") have to herd the steer around the ring twice before coming in for the bone-crunching smash against the wall.

The Puerto Montt ring is high on a ridge overlooking sun-drenched Lake Llanquihue in south central Chile. On the far side of the deep blue water is the brooding crest of the Osorno volcano. The shouting rodeo crowd makes up for the lack of smoke and fire from the volcano, which has been dormant for years. The ring is set in a natural bowl, just outside this provincial capital of 87,000 citizens.

Federico lives about 600 miles (966 kilometers) south of Santiago, the capital of Chile. His father is one of the area's top rodeo riders. The family and their riding friends go to Santiago every spring for the national rodeo championships. Each year, someone from their town comes back with trophies and ribbons. Someday, Federico hopes, he will be one of those lucky heroes.

A huaso isn't a professional. He is usually a farmer or rancher who enjoys showing off his horsemanship. Each wears a colorful

8

A huaso's tools include the spurs (left) and a hornless saddle (right).

shoulder cape called a *manta*. His spurs have rowels that seem as big as windmills. The rowels are the circular disks that are used to prod the sides of the horse to make it go faster. The huaso wears thigh-high leather leggings called *pierneras* that fit over his riding boots. The pierneras protect the huaso's legs when galloping through thick brush, much like the chaps worn by Mexican and Yankee cowboys.

A Chilean saddle doesn't have a horn in the front, so the rider doesn't have anything but air to grab if a grumpy steer decides to butt into his horse. The huaso has learned to sit easy in his saddle, because he has been riding since he was a little boy.

Chile's first rodeos took place in the 1600s, long before Chile was an independent country. At first, the rodeos concluded round-up time and were part of the counting of herds and branding of calves. Eventually, they became contests in which the huaso could display his bravery in the arena.

Federico's family has participated in rodeos for generations. His Spanish ancestors settled in Chile three hundred years ago, so

Antofagasta

Valparaíso   Santiago

Puerto
Montt

Strait of
Magellan

Tierra del Fuego

Comic books for sale in Santiago

Federico has a lot of tradition to remember. But today, he simply loves the smell of the barbecuing beef drifting down from the outdoor grill above the arena.

There's nothing better than saddling his horse and riding into the ring. What could be more fun than talking over the events of the day with his cousin Raúl? They practice at home a great deal. They want to be rodeo stars.

Not all young people of Chile have the chance to be huasos. But there are many things for them to do, regardless of where they live.

To the north of Puerto Montt, Damián sells comic books on the steps of the Popular Arts Museum in Santiago. Donald Duck and Mickey Mouse are the most popular characters. Damián is a mixture of Indian, Spanish, and Italian heritages. He is called a "mestizo." His dark eyes are bright when he urges you to buy his magazines. They are all printed in Spanish, which is the official language of Chile.

The port of Valparaíso

Damián lives in a small house at the edge of the city. His father sells cheese from a flatbed wagon along Santiago's main streets. At the end of the day, Damián and his father walk home together. They are very tired.

Rose's home is in Valparaíso. Her parents are Arabs who came to Chile from the Middle East after World War II. Thousands of other Arabs live in Valparaíso, which is the principal port of Chile. Like Rose's parents, most Arabs work in the textile mills here. Rose thinks of herself as Chilean, however. She loves playing on the hills overlooking the harbor. It is exciting to take the *ascensores,* the cogwheel streetcars, up and down the hills. It is much faster than walking.

The mining town of El Salvador (right) is a major producer of copper.
Ore (left) is being unloaded into a crusher.

A desert stretches across most of the northern tip of Chile. Leonor's father operates a huge scoop shovel in the open pit copper mine at Chuquicamata. It is the largest mine of its kind in the world. Leonor lives in an apartment on the outskirts of Antofagasta, the biggest city in the region. It hardly ever rains here, but Leonor grows some flowers outside her house, being careful not to waste the tapwater. After school, she takes care of her little brother, Tony, and helps her mother around the house. She also practices her violin. "Perhaps if I study hard enough, I can go to Santiago and join the symphony there," she tells herself.

More than 2,000 miles (3,219 kilometers) to the south, at the other end of the country, Felipe herds sheep with his father and two older brothers. The wind whips the storm clouds above their heads, blowing in from the ocean. The Estrecho de Magallanes— the Strait of Magellan—is not far away. Below the strait is the very

Sheep on their way to the shearing sheds

tip of Chile, a rough, rocky place called Tierra del Fuego (Land of Fire). Early explorers thought they saw signal fires on this island and thus gave it its name. Felipe has heard those stories but isn't sure. He thinks the fires might be the eyes of dancing ghosts. "The Ona Indians used to live there," he says. You can believe Felipe's tales if you stand on the rocky cliffs at night, with only the stars overhead and the friendly sheep for companions.

You would see this diversity in Chile if you visited Federico, Damián, Rose, Leonor, and Felipe. Chile is a long, thin stretch of land whose people come from many different ethnic backgrounds. If you hadn't expected this diversity, Chile will be full of surprises for you. It is very different from other South American nations. Many traditions have blended in this land, creating an exciting atmosphere. Let's see for ourselves. Join us now on a short reading trip to the enchanting land of Chile, one of the most European of all Latin nations.

Above: Islands in the Chilean archipelago
Below: "Robinson Crusoe's island" in the Juan Fernández Islands

Chapter 2

NARROW NATION WITH
A DISTINCT LANDSCAPE

Chile is one of the narrowest countries in the world. It is 56 miles (90 kilometers) wide at its thinnest point in the south and barely 236 miles (380 kilometers) across at its widest point in the north. However, it is very long. Chile's northern border, which touches Peru, is 2,650 miles (4,265 kilometers) from its southern tip at Tierra del Fuego. In addition to Peru, Chile is bordered on the northeast by Bolivia and on the east by Argentina. The Pacific Ocean forms the western boundary, and the Atlantic touches a tip on the southeast.

Many island possessions dot the ocean like runaway freckles. Among these are the Juan Fernández and Diego Ramírez islands and Easter Island. One of the Juan Fernández group, located 400 miles (644 kilometers) off the Chilean mainland, was the refuge of Alexander Selkirk. His ordeal after being shipwrecked on an island became the basis for the famous book by Daniel Defoe called *Robinson Crusoe*.

Easter Island lies 2,300 miles (3,701 kilometers) from Chile. It is a dot of land that has a fascinating history. It was discovered by

Gigantic statues on Easter Island (left). Magellanic penguins nest north of Punta Arenas (right).

Dutch explorers on Easter Sunday, 1722. That's how the island was named. Many giant statues are on Easter Island (also known as Rapa Nui). Nobody knows where these "moais" came from or how they got there. Some are seventy feet (21 meters) tall and even the smallest weighs at least ten tons (8 metric tons). Archaeologists think the statues might have been used for ancestor worship by early Polynesians who lived there. But they are not sure.

Other islands belonging to Chile rise like mountaintops in the passage between South America and Antarctica. In fact, they actually were mountains before the rumbling and shaking of the earth caused the valleys around them to be flooded by the raging sea eons ago. A vast ice sheet also covered this region, pushing down the rock and crunching it to form the up-and-down landscape that can be seen today. Chile also claims 482,500 square miles (1,249,675 square kilometers) of Antarctica. Some scientists live on that frozen continent, conducting experiments and keeping the penguins company.

Sparse vegetation in the semidesert near Caldera

Counting all its territory except Antarctica, Chile owns some 292,058 square miles (756,430 square kilometers) of land. It is one of the smallest South American countries. Only Ecuador, Paraguay, and Uruguay are smaller.

Chile can be divided into at least five distinct sections. First is the northern desert, consisting of dry brown hills and sparse vegetation. Leonor and her family live here. This region is rich in minerals. The Atacama Desert stretches across the entire north country. It is the driest desert in the world. Rain has never been known to fall on some parts of this barren land. Not even the hearty cactus grows there.

In a few desert valleys, however, there are underground springs which water the oases. Many of the mining communities in the north receive lifegiving water by pipelines from the Andes.

Next comes the semidesert, where irrigation is now being used to boost agricultural production. The third zone includes a fertile valley that stretches from the city of Illapel to Concepción. Rose and Damián live in this region. Numerous farms and vineyards here produce much of Chile's food.

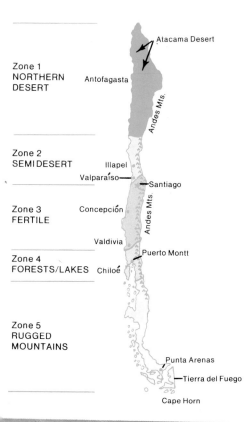

Zone 1
NORTHERN
DESERT

Zone 2
SEMIDESERT

Zone 3
FERTILE

Zone 4
FORESTS/LAKES

Zone 5
RUGGED
MOUNTAINS

Atacama Desert

Antofagasta

Andes Mts.

Illapel
Valparaíso — Santiago
Concepción
Andes Mts.
Valdivia
Puerto Montt
Chiloé

Punta Arenas
Tierra del Fuego
Cape Horn

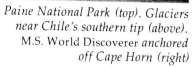

Paine National Park (top). Glaciers near Chile's southern tip (above). M.S. World Discoverer anchored off Cape Horn (right)

The fourth zone, where Federico lives, is heavily forested, dotted with huge lakes and crisscrossed by hundreds of rivers. This area is great for fishing and hiking. The fifth zone, which is the most southern, ranges from the island of Chiloé, just south of Puerto Montt, to Cape Horn at the tip of the continent. It is almost unpopulated because of the rugged terrain. Except for some people who work in small towns, most of the population are sheepherders like Felipe, timber cutters, fishermen, and farmers. This is the Chilean archipelago, complete with glaciers, channels, steep cliffs, and islands. The climate is constantly cold and stormy. Atlantic Chile, a small section of land along the Magellan Strait to the east of the Andes, is here as well.

Chile can also be divided from east to west by drawing parallel lines up and down the length of the country. The interior consists of the peaks and valleys of the Andes Mountains. The range has many volcanoes and towering snow-covered ridges.

Chile's Ojos del Salado mountain is the second highest peak in South America, soaring 22,539 feet (6,870 meters) into the blue skies. The highest peak in the Western Hemisphere is Mount Aconcagua, on the border of Chile and Argentina, which rises 22,889 feet (6,976 meters).

The center zone consists of a long valley between the Andes and the coastal mountain ranges. Seventy percent of Chile's population lives in these lowlands. The outer zone incorporates the coastal mountains and the seacoast.

This long, bony country lies atop one of the most active earthquake zones in the world. With regularity, the ground wiggles and squirms in tune with Mother Nature's wild rhythm.

Some geologists think that South America and Africa once formed a single landmass while the earth was still in its infancy.

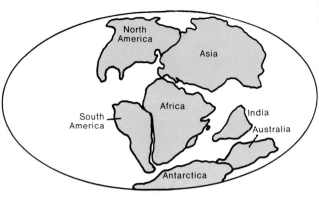

In 1960 and 1985 massive earthquakes ravaged Chile, leaving thousands homeless.

As the land cooled, these two huge chunks drifted apart. The westerly movement of what is now South America caused some of the surface to buckle and fold into a high ridge, the coastal mountains of Chile. These are at least 500 million years old and are worn down by rain and wind. However, a hundred million years ago, scientists say that another ridge was formed inland from the sea. Earthquakes and volcanoes shook the landscape for a long time, giving birth to the Andes.

This mountain building is still going on, although most of the wildest activity occurred twenty-five million years ago. But at least one earthquake occurs every day somewhere in this roller-coaster land. In 1906, Valparaíso was demolished for the fifth time in two hundred years. If you lived there, you might wonder about the city's nickname, "Valley of Paradise."

Ten days in 1960 were even more devastating. Southern Chile was shaken by a terrible earthquake as new mountains rumbled, islands were formed, and lakes opened up. Giant tidal waves swept inland and killed thousands of people.

Villarrica Volcano (left) and Llaima Volcano (right) in the Lake District

In March 1985 another earthquake shook central Chile, killing more than one hundred people and injuring more than two thousand. Houses, churches, and other structures collapsed, leaving tens of thousands of people without homes. Cities hardest hit included Santiago, Valparaíso, Viña del Mar, and other coastal towns.

Volcanoes can also be dangerous. However, most are in sparsely populated regions in the north along the border between Bolivia and northern Argentina. But people still keep a watchful eye on Oyahue, Socompa, and Lastarria, three of the more active peaks. Then there's Llaima in the south, still spitting smoke and steam at regular intervals.

One of the world's hot spots is the province of Antofagasta. In this province there are at least twelve volcanoes that are 17,000 feet (5,182 meters) high.

The Chileans don't let all this turmoil of the earth bother them. They've learned to live with the ups and downs of nature. They love their land because of its incredible beauty and variety.

One of the prettiest sections of Chile is the Lake District south

Kayaking in the Fuy River (left) and Bío-Bío River (right).
Araucaria trees line the Bío-Bío shore.

of Santiago. With the views of the snowcapped Andes, the district has gained the nickname of "The South American Switzerland." Lake Todos los Santos, Lake Llanquihue, and Lake Villarrica are very well known. Many resorts surround these big lakes and the smaller ones that dot the countryside.

Chileans have a natural kinship with water. It is everywhere in their country. The rivers run westward from the Andes and empty into the sea. Only the Imperial River can be navigated because most of the others are too shallow and dangerous. The Loa River in the north is the longest in the country, flowing for about 300 miles (483 kilometers). Other well-known rivers are the Bío-Bío, Aconcagua, Palena, Copiapó, and Maipo. In addition to providing irrigation waters, the Chilean rivers are used to produce hydroelectric power.

Chile's climate ranges from tropical to polar, depending on the latitude. The many mountains also affect the climate. They act as "climatic shields," preventing rain clouds from forming over the desert. The cold Humboldt Current runs along the coast, preventing extreme temperatures even in the northern wastes.

Since Chile is south of the equator, its seasons are exactly opposite those in the Northern Hemisphere. When it is summer in North America, for instance, it is winter in Chile. December and January are the warmest months; July and August are the coldest. Generally, Chile has a moderate climate.

According to Indian legends, Chile was formed when two serpents crawling across the broad, flat land met. One serpent was named Kai Kai. All the smaller creatures ran away from him in terror. The other serpent was Trey Trey. The other animals would move out of his way, but they weren't afraid of him. Eventually, the two snakes faced each other. They had a terrible battle, knocking over hills and flattening out the land like they were rolling pins.

Kai Kai won the battle, but he hissed so much he created an ocean. To save himself and the other animals, Trey Trey piled mounds of earth into mountains to divert the water. He and the other animals crawled up on the ridges. Some were not strong enough and fell into the sea to become fish. The animals who climbed the fastest and highest became humans. After the flood, the humans scrambled down from their refuge and found a fertile valley between Trey Trey's mountains and Kai Kai's ocean. Here they settled, calling themselves the Mapuche. *Che* is the Indian word for people and *mapu* means land. It is easy to imagine serpents battling over their territories. Whenever a tremor occurs even now, you can almost see the thrashing snakes.

Above: Andes Mountains above Uspallata Pass
Below: Grand Falls of the Payne River in southern Chile

Chapter 3
INDIANS TO INDEPENDENCE

No one is sure how the first people arrived in South America. Probably Indians trickled down from the north over thousands and thousands of years. Imagine the difficulties they faced when they finally reached the Andes. Towering cliffs, fast flowing rivers, freezing weather—no wonder they told legends about Kai Kai and Trey Trey.

The Indians' stories about the "first humans" might have originated in that dim past. It would have been a good way to describe how their ancestors climbed over the Andes. However, some researchers claim that the early Indians might have been descendants of Polynesian sailors who journeyed across the Pacific. As you can see, there are many theories and folktales about these early people.

One thing is certain, however. Indians lived in Chile at least ten thousand years ago. Archaeologists have found remains of burial sites, ancient camps, and many artifacts dating back thousands of years. However, none of these Indians had developed as complex a civilization as did the Maya, Inca, and Aztec farther to the north.

Arica-La Paz Railroad winds through the Atacama Desert.

Perhaps life in Chile was too precarious. Days were spent searching for wild game and edible plants. Northern Chile, in the Atacama Desert, was a desolate place, almost like the moon. So the tribes who lived there were nomads—they moved from place to place searching for water and food.

Some Indians did eventually settle down. Most lived along the seacoast where they could hunt for porpoise and fish in the shallow water along the shore. Remains of villages and fields have been found near the mouths of rivers, indicating that some of those early people were farmers. Stone walls surrounded their tiny communities. Other tribes must have attacked them often for such defenses to be necessary.

Other Indians, such as the Diaguita, lived farther inland. They are believed to have come overland from Argentina and occupied the semidesert between the coast and the mountains. They herded llamas and alpacas, two odd-looking animals whose wool was used for clothes. Both animals are related to the camel, but do not have humps.

Llamas (left) have been domesticated for use as pack animals.
An Indian tepee (right) near the Puerto Williams Museum

The Inca were the major enemy of these Chilean Indians. These fierce warriors lived in Peru to the north of Chile, and had a highly developed culture. They subdued many of the desert tribes and demanded that they pay tribute. The Inca might have learned some irrigation techniques from the people they conquered.

Farther south lived the Yamanes, Chonos, and Alacalufe Indians. They were even more primitive than the people who lived in the desert. They lived on islands or along the seacoast. They would make boats from hollowed-out logs, bark, or animal skins. Instead of living in permanent villages, these Indians made huts of twigs and branches. They would often move in search of food, so it did not matter if their homes were not very solid.

The Ona Indians lived on Tierra del Fuego and were the most southern of all the Chilean Indians. They would eat shellfish, small rodents, and water birds. They were very primitive. The Ona did not even live in huts, but propped skins on poles to protect themselves from the wind.

Of all the Indians, the Mapuche were the most widespread and advanced. They had numerous subtribes who lived throughout

*Mapuche mother and baby (left). Ruins of
the ancient city of Lasana (right), built by Peruvian Inca*

Chile in many small communities. Their houses were called rukas.
These houses were originally made of skins. Eventually, they were
made of mud which dried in the sun to become as hard as cement.
Living in a ruka was like living in a blockhouse. These rukas were
sometimes thirty feet (9 meters) long. Often they were even
longer, housing many members of the same family. It was very
crowded, but inside the ruka everyone was safe. Three to eight
rukas made up a village.

The Mapuche believed spirits were everywhere, and they looked
for divine intervention in all aspects of their lives. Their medicine
women were very powerful and were as important as chiefs.

The Mapuche were very warlike. Captured enemies would be
tortured before they were killed. When there weren't any
neighbors to fight, the Mapuche would battle among themselves.
Sometimes, families would fight families in the same village. The
Mapuche would use human bones as flutes and human skulls for
drinking cups.

Portuguese navigator Ferdinand Magellan (left); fjord north of the Strait of Magellan (right)

Only the Inca were strong enough to challenge the Mapuche. However, even the Inca could not keep the wild Chilean warriors under strict control. The Mapuche would hide in the woods and attack Inca war parties.

This was the situation in Chile when the first Europeans arrived. In 1520 the brave Portuguese explorer Ferdinand Magellan sailed through the strait that would eventually be named after him. He was seeking a sea route from Europe to the rich spice islands in the Pacific, so he didn't stay in Chile. Magellan's storm-tossed ships had a hard time getting around the rocky tip of South America. He was more concerned with sailing safely through the strait than with landing and colonizing. But Magellan probably did see the signal fires of the Ona Indians, so he knew the land was occupied.

Spanish conquistadors Diego de Almagro (left) and Francisco Pizarro (right)

Four years later, Spanish colonists from Panama headed south in search of gold. Soon, the Spanish soldier Francisco Pizarro conquered the Inca in Peru and decided to send exploring parties into Chile. He thought there might be even richer treasures there.

Diego de Almagro, another conquistador (as the conquering Spanish soldiers were called), was ordered to find the best route to Chile. He figured there would not be much to discover in Chile's great northern desert, so he moved his troops over the Andes, starting his expedition in 1535. He had 500 Spaniards and 15,000 Indians—including some Inca—among his men. The Inca had told the Spaniards about the tribes in "Chile." The meaning of this Indian name is not clear, but it probably meant "the end of the world" or "land's end" in their language.

Many of the Spaniards and their Indian allies died of starvation and thirst before they got very far. They battled the Mapuche and discovered that these fierce warriors were certainly tough fighters. Almagro turned back. After two years, he and his men finally straggled into Peru. The survivors were nicknamed "The Men of Chile" after their horrible ordeal.

Even before Almagro's expedition, he and Pizarro hated and feared each other. Pizarro knew that Almagro and his men would want some reward for all the troubles they had encountered. But Pizarro was too greedy to give rewards. Instead, he had Almagro put to death, claiming his captain was guilty of treason. Almagro was innocent of the charges, a fact remembered by the Men of Chile and by Almagro's son. Three years later, they assassinated Pizarro.

But a year before he died, Pizarro sent another explorer into Chile. This was Pedro de Valdivia. Valdivia was not afraid, despite the terrible stories told by the Men of Chile. But he listened to their grim tales and decided to travel along the coast rather than cross the treacherous mountains or the desert.

Valdivia killed almost all the Indians he met on his way down the coast because he did not want them attacking him from the rear once he moved on. In February, 1541, Valdivia reached a hill near the Rio Mapocho. This spot would be easy to defend from all the angry Indian tribes who had heard about his cruelty. He established a fort on the site, naming it Santiago (the City of St. James).

Valdivia gave the surrounding land to his officers. According to the custom of the day, this also meant that they could collect tribute from the natives who lived on their land. Since the Indians had little material wealth, they paid by working. But it took more than three hundred years before the brave Indians were subjugated. Their resistance became known as the "Wars of Arauco." Spanish King Philip II said that this long, bloody struggle was "costing me the flower of my Guzmans." He meant that the Indian turmoil was sacrificing Spain's best military men.

The Chilean Indians, especially the Mapuche, were unreliable

Mapuche Indians near Nueva-Imperial, west of Temuco

laborers. This meant that the Spaniards themselves had to work in the fields, although most of the mining was done by Indians. Many settlers in Central and South America brought Spanish women from home to be their wives. However, many of the Spanish soldiers stayed in Chile and took Indian wives.

The Spaniards founded other towns around the country, which were eventually populated largely by mestizos, the mixed-blood descendants of the Spaniards and Indians. Many black slaves were brought to Chile in chains. These slaves eventually married into other Chilean ethnic groups. Today there is no trace of their culture.

*Pedro de Valdivia,
conqueror of Chile*

Valdivia had a hard time recruiting settlers from Peru. No one would listen to Valdivia's messengers who praised Chile's rich soil and its opportunities to make a fortune. The Peruvian Spaniards remembered what had happened to the Men of Chile! They were afraid of the rigorous life they would encounter in Chile. So Valdivia himself decided to go to Lima, the capital of Peru, hoping to talk people into joining him. He arrived in time to help in a revolution that overthrew Gonzalo Pizarro, the cruel half brother of Francisco Pizarro. Valdivia's help made him popular with the rebels. But few people wanted to leave their good life in Peru to follow him to a land full of angry Indians.

Among Valdivia's Indian servants was a young man named Lautaro. He was very observant and watched how the Spaniards fought. Lautaro eventually escaped and fled back to his tribe. He became a war chief and successfully battled the Spaniards using their own tactics. Valdivia was captured by his former prisoner and tortured. According to legend, the Spaniard was boiled alive in molten gold. However, he probably was beaten to death.

In the ensuing years, the Spaniards fought other Indian heroes, such as Caupolicán and Galvarino. Because of the tenacity and bravery of the Indians, the conquistadors had to accept a frontier line along the Bío-Bío River. The Spaniards stayed north of the river and the Indians remained in the south for several generations.

The distant Spanish king appointed governors for Chile who also had the title of captain-general. These men ruled as independent dictators, although they were supposed to be under the control of the king's representative, or viceroy, in Lima. Only the Catholic church was able to exert any authority over these politician-soldiers. The priests argued for better treatment of the Indians and mestizos on the haciendas, the vast estates owned by the Spaniards. Eventually, some reforms were initiated. Schools and hospitals were set up for the workers.

In the 1600s, the Mapuche again raided the Spanish settlements. In 1641, Chile's Governor Francisco Lopez de Zúñiga asked for a peace conference with the war chiefs. A truce was established. As the territory quieted again, the old aristocratic families acquired more and more land. Some families had more land than there were workers, but the rich owners would not allow the peasants and the Indians to farm their own plots.

Over the years, Chile became more independent and resisted the orders given by the viceroy in Peru. After listening to years of grumbling from his Chilean subjects, Spanish King Charles III finally gave them more voice in their own affairs. But he refused to let them go off on their own. However, the Chileans still wanted to be completely free from Peru. Besides, Spain was so far away that nobody paid much attention to the king.

Events in Europe began to have more impact on the New World. Napoleon Bonaparte of France seized power in 1799 and

Statue of Bernardo O'Higgins, liberator of Chile, stands near the port of Punta Arenas.

began a series of wars. As all this was going on, a young man named Bernardo O'Higgins was studying in Europe. He was the son of an Irish man (who was governor of Chile and later viceroy of Peru) and a Chilean woman. While away at school, O'Higgins met many revolutionaries. He dreamed about bringing freedom to his own country. He returned home in 1802 and talked about independence among his people. Many of them supported O'Higgins.

Napoleon invaded Spain in 1808 and put his own brother on the throne after jailing Spanish King Fernando VII. The Chileans did not want to give their allegiance to the French. So on September 18, 1810, they formed a *junta,* a group of nine men from Santiago who would help the Chilean captain-general govern until Fernando regained his throne. Then, the junta reasoned, Chile could go back to the old ways. That date is remembered now as National Independence Day, marking the first government of Chile set up by Chileans.

The junta called for a National Congress, but it took a long time for the aristocrats to assemble in Santiago. In the meantime, some citizens of the city of Concepción revolted, declaring their independence from the junta. During the resulting confusion, José Miguel Carrera, a popular military officer who had fought the French in Spain, saw an opportunity to seize power. He attacked forces loyal to the junta. Then he declared himself dictator, retook Concepción, disbanded the National Congress, and put many of his relatives in power.

All this made O'Higgins very angry. He helped overthrow Carrera in 1813 and became leader of the Chilean revolutionaries. The viceroy of Peru sent armies into Chile to put down the revolt. O'Higgins and his followers were defeated and fled to Argentina, where they allied themselves with a friend O'Higgins had met while a student in Spain. This man was José de San Martín.

The Peruvian royalists were harsh rulers. Most of them were very attached to Spain. They didn't like the Chileans. Soon Chileans of all social classes were looking for a liberator. Napoleon was defeated in 1813 and the Spanish king was back in power. The king didn't like what the Chileans had done by setting up a junta and a Congress, so he supported the viceroy from Peru.

But by now San Martín had defeated the Spaniards in Argentina. The time was ripe for revolution in other Spanish colonies in South America. He and O'Higgins agreed to attack Chile. They began crossing the Andes in January, 1817. Since this was the Chilean summer, the passes were relatively clear of snow. Yet it was very hard to cross the high mountain passes because the thin air was difficult to breathe. Many soldiers died as they struggled along the rugged way. They had to push and pull their cannons and wagons by hand because the trails were too steep for

José de San Martín's army crossing the Andes in Chile's war of independence

teams. But most of the army made it safely, although it was ragged, sick, and hungry. The Spaniards were surprised; they hadn't expected an attack from over the Andes.

Led by O'Higgins and San Martín the revolutionaries defeated the loyalists in a fierce battle at Chacabuco on February 12, 1817. Within days, the victors entered Santiago to the cheers of the Chileans. The Spaniards did not give up easily, however. They attacked again and again. The decisive fight took place on the plains of Maipú on March 19, 1818. O'Higgins and San Martín were almost beaten, but they were able to rally their tattered forces in time.

This was the last major battle of the Chilean revolution; however, pockets of Spanish troops held out for years. The fort of San Antonio on the southern island of Chiloé wasn't captured until 1826! The Chileans didn't care. They were free at last. Chile was no longer a colony. It was an independent republic.

Chapter 4

MOVING TOWARD TODAY

Independence was exciting. Bernardo O'Higgins was named Supreme Director of Chile by José de San Martín, who went on to carry the revolution to Peru. However, even with the Spaniards gone, the social structure did not change a great deal with the new order of power in Chile. Still in control were the military and the aristocracy. Although this was not much of an issue at the time, it was a very different situation from the American and French revolutions, when the old order was overthrown.

The aristocracy had ruled through municipal councils during the days of Spanish rule. It did the same through the newly formed Congress. The military was on hand to keep an eye on things.

To help San Martín in his fight in Peru, O'Higgins asked a Scotsman named Thomas Cochrane to form a Chilean navy. Cochrane took command of a motley fleet of old ships that had been purchased from the United States and England. He ferried San Martín's army to Peru and kept the royalists from attacking Chile by sea. In this way, he aided the new Chilean government.

However, O'Higgins was a better general than a governor. He made enemies because he was so stubborn. He angered many of the aristocrats because he abolished titles of nobility. He even did

Diego Portales, father of Chile's constitution

away with bullfights, which were a prime source of entertainment for the rich people. He brought in teachers from England to help in schools for the poor. This angered the clergy, who had previously controlled the educational system.

Another revolution broke out because the rich and powerful Chileans did not like what O'Higgins was doing. But O'Higgins was able to crush his opponents. The powerful landowners banded together, however, and demanded that O'Higgins resign. He finally agreed to step down and subsequently went into exile. He then went to Peru to help his friend San Martín. After a long and eventful political and military career, O'Higgins died in 1842.

Another junta followed O'Higgins. But the officers were weak leaders and poor rulers. Everyone was afraid of another revolution. Diego Portales, a member of the Conservative political party, gained sole power in 1830. He set up a militia loyal only to himself, the aristocrats, and wealthy businessmen. This provided a counterbalance to the army. Under his direction, Roman Catholicism became the state church, which made the clergy happy. Although Portales was very conservative and authoritarian, he did direct the writing of a Chilean constitution which remained in effect for many years. His influence is still alive in Chilean politics.

Yet the turmoil of Chilean politics eventually even caught up with Portales. He was shot to death by some soldiers who opposed his reforms.

For the next thirty years the Liberal party was in power. They changed many of the things that Portales and his followers had favored. The conservatives and the church again were put on the defensive and lost some of their privileges. Those groups out of power wanted power. There still wasn't peace.

In 1866 the Spaniards made one last attempt to regain control of Chile. They bombarded Valparaíso but were driven off by the Chilean navy. That was the last time the Spaniards attempted anything like that.

Chile looked outward and began expanding its exports. Rich silver deposits were discovered; the nitrate deposits and other mineral wealth in the Antofagasta and Tarapacá regions were developed. Administration of this region was shared among Chile, Bolivia, and Peru. But the Chilean rulers wanted the entire territory. They wanted only the Chileans to get rich. So they declared war on their neighbors. This "War of the Pacific" raged from 1879 to 1883. Even though it was very serious and many people were killed, some jokesters called it "The Fertilizer War" and worse names because nitrates were also used as a base for crop fertilizers.

The Chilean troops fought well, defeating their rivals in almost every battle. They even occupied Lima, Peru for a time. When peace finally arrived, the Chileans received the fabulous mineral treasure troves in the north and northeast. Chile then took advantage of its new mineral wealth and gradually moved from an agricultural economy to that of a mining country exporting nitrates and copper.

Typical thatched roofs on a Mapuche farm

One surprise lay in store for the landowners and rich of Chile. The common people didn't want to return to the old days when they had little say in their government. Ex-soldiers and new immigrants demanded more liberty. They saw how things were in the outside world. They wanted a share of real freedom.

Few wished to return to work in the fields of the big haciendas. Thousands moved south, over the Bío-Bío River into Indian territory. It was almost like the settling of the West in the United States. French, Italians, Swiss, English, Germans, and even Spanish Basques arrived from Europe. Many of them flooded into the newly opened lands along with the native Chileans. Of course, the Indians resisted angrily. The centuries-old peace treaty was shattered. The frontier was in flames.

The Indians were defeated this time and were forced to live on reservations where disease and alcoholism decimated the proud people. Most could not or did not want to adapt to new ways. Only a few Indians remained by the end of the 1800s. Again it was the Mapuche who were able to adapt the best; their descendants still live in southern Chile where many are now farmers.

José Manuel Balmaceda

The early governments of Chile didn't really care what was happening to the poor. The middle class of small businessmen and factory owners, however, grew politically and socially stronger as their investments in the mines paid off. José Manuel Balmaceda, a Liberal, gained control of the government in 1886 and started many public works improvements.

Although he was honest, many of his supporters were not. They stole public money and became rich. By 1890, angry voters elected more Conservatives to the National Congress who refused to agree to Balmaceda's requests for more money. He declared he would rule without the help of Congress.

The legislature turned around and voted to remove the president. Jorge Montt, a Chilean naval officer, was named to replace him. This led to a civil war in 1891. Montt quickly gained control of the northern mines, effectively shutting off any revenue to Balmaceda and his supporters. Congress eventually defeated the Liberals in the bloody struggle, which ended with the battle of Placilla, near Viña del Mar. Balmaceda sought refuge in the Argentinian ministry in Santiago, where he took his own life.

After the war, the Congress increased its power and made the the president a mere political figurehead. For the next thirty years Congress would rule Chile. During this time, the country was at peace. In 1904, a large statue called "Christ of the Andes" was placed above Uspallata Pass as a memorial to the calm conclusion of a border dispute with Argentina. The statue still stands there.

World War I made Chile wealthy. Everyone needed the nitrate in order to make gunpowder. The rich grew richer. But the future did not look pleasant. The Allied navies, led by England and the United States, blockaded the German ports. They prevented Chilean products from being unloaded. As the war dragged on, the Germans in Europe were forced to develop synthetic nitrate. To add to Chile's problem, the new nitrate substitutes were cheaper to produce. It wasn't long before other countries were doing the same thing. The demand for nitrate fell.

The middle class turned more to socialistic and anarchistic ideals following the war as they lost many of their markets for natural resources. They grew angry when they saw how the money was going only to a relatively few people. Labor unrest spread as the international demand fell for copper and nitrate. Arturo Alessandri Palma squeaked into the presidency in 1920, and for the first time the middle class was in power. Alessandri was called the "Lion of Tarapacá" because he had been a champion of the people in his home district. As president, he tried to improve conditions for the workers. But this activity, plus the fact that the Congress voted itself a higher salary, angered army officers who had fallen behind in their pay. A revolution followed and Alessandri was deposed. He fled to Italy.

In a strange twist, however, he was brought back by the military when they found no other politician who could govern as well. The old constitution was replaced, the presidential powers that had been taken away by Congress were given back, and the people were allowed to vote directly for their chief executive.

Once Alessandri was back in power, his activities frightened the military, who again lost faith in him. He resigned in 1925 and retired to Italy. Colonel Carlos Ibáñez del Campo was elected president and made himself dictator. He was a harsh ruler and was not reelected in 1931 when his term ended. There was street fighting in Santiago and Ibáñez had to flee to Argentina, the same country that had harbored so many other Chilean politicians in the past.

The depression of the 1930s brought hard times for Chile. The mines closed, businesses failed, and the ports fell into disrepair. To his surprise, Alessandri was called back to office for another try at stabilizing Chile. His political views at the time were influenced by Benito Mussolini, who was the Fascist dictator of Italy. However, Alessandri was able to put Chile's economy on the highway to recovery. He encouraged trade and got many people back to work. But he still wasn't popular because he was very harsh in dealing with political opponents.

After Alessandri, Chileans elected several governments that were politically center and left-of-center. These were called the Radical governments. From 1938 to 1958 they did much to promote local industry and help the poor people. The state became very powerful. It became the center for economic development. But sometimes the state helped the sectors in need more than it could afford. This caused an inflation in the economy that is still a problem in Chile.

Pedro Aguirre Cerda was president after Alessandri. He belonged to the *Frente Popular,* or Popular Front. Rather than favoring the left or right (Liberal or Conservative parties), Cerda believed that the center was the best. He helped Chile remain neutral during World War II.

Chilean president Gabriel González Videla (left) addressing the Organization of American States. Government troops (right) escort prisoners in Santiago after a 1938 Nazi revolt failed.

A few people in the German community backed the Nazis. But most supported the Allies and helped identify spies who were causing trouble in their country. After the war, Chile helped found the United Nations, taking a place as a leading voice for South America on the international scene.

Gabriel González Videla was elected president in 1946. He wanted to experiment with governmental reforms and brought some Communists into his cabinet. After a while, however, he banned the Communist party because he feared it was organizing to overthrow his government.

Carlos Ibáñez del Campo, who had been in power in 1927, was elected president again in 1952. His supporters came from both the left and the right. By the end of his term in 1958, the Chilean middle class was well represented in the government. Nevertheless, the rich were still getting richer and the poor, poorer.

The next president was Jorge Alessandri Rodríguez, son of the "Lion of Tarapacá." Unlike his father, the son was a conservative, and was pressured by leftist groups throughout his term.

About this time, a new type of center party appeared on the scene—the Christian Democratic party. This party, like the leftists, believed in changing social structures by redistributing the land. In 1964, the Christian Democrats won the elections, under the leadership of Eduardo Frei Montalva. Although he was popular with the voters, he never really satisfied either side of the political spectrum during his tenure from 1964 to 1970.

Frei instituted a series of reforms that he called "revolution in freedom." He initiated agrarian reforms and nationalized the copper industry. He also improved education, bringing Chile to the highest mass education level in Latin America. But the left did not think he moved far enough or fast enough. In 1970, a Marxist coalition was elected under the presidency of Salvador Allende Gossens. Allende had the support of three other political parties, in addition to his own Socialists.

Allende continued what Frei had begun. He broke up the hacienda estates so the poorer people could have more land, pushing the agrarian reform far beyond what the country could stand. He nationalized industries and sought closer ties with Communist countries. His activities frightened many Chileans.

The country was soon divided into pro-Allende and anti-Allende factions, and there were street battles between the two sides. No one seemed to want to work together. The economy was in a shambles and outrageous inflation levels cut the value of Chilean money.

The military was neutral at first but it eventually pressured Allende to slow down in his rush to make Chile a socialist

Presidential palace in flames (left) as the government of President Allende is overthrown. Demonstrators in Santiago (right) hurl rocks at police during violent protests against Allende's policies.

country. He allowed some officers to serve in his cabinet, yet the economic and political chaos continued.

The disgruntled army led a revolt that deposed Allende in September, 1973. There was much fighting throughout the country, which culminated in a gun battle in the halls of the presidential palace. It is said that Allende committed suicide as the soldiers burst into his office. But some people believe he was killed by the troops. Many Allende supporters died in the coup and hundreds fled the country. Thousands were arrested.

General Augusto Pinochet Ugarte took firm control of the new junta and promised a more conservative economic policy. He said he would favor closer ties with Western nations. But Chile's economic troubles continued. To consolidate his power and bring more order to the situation, Pinochet assumed the position as head of state in 1974. He closed Congress and outlawed political parties.

On September 11, 1980, Chilean voters approved a new constitution that concentrated power in the presidency. The president could then be directly elected by the voters, but the document provided for an eight-year "transition" period in which

Pinochet was to hold the chief office. Under the constitution, the junta is allowed to exercise legislative power in place of a Congress. Eventually, a bicameral (two-house) legislative body is to be reestablished.

Pinochet was eventually officially designated president and took office on March 11, 1981, amid much pomp and ceremony. There was a ceremony at the national cathedral, attended by numerous dignitaries and church leaders. The ceremony was followed by a parade to Moneda Palace, Chile's traditional government house.

Navy, air force, and army officers now act as governors of each of the twelve regions of Chile and the metropolitan area of Santiago. The regional arrangement replaced the old system of twenty-five provinces that existed prior to 1974. The new regional names are: Tarapacá, Antofagasta, Atacama, Coquimbo, Aconcagua, Libertador General Bernardo O'Higgins, Maule, Bío-Bío, La Araucania, Los Lagos, Aisén del General Carlos Ibáñez del Campo, and Magallanes y Antártica Chilena. Even after the transition period ends, the constitution ensures that the military is guaranteed a permanent political role.

Under the current system, political parties and unions are prohibited, or "in recess." The press is regulated as well. The president has retained special powers that let him arrest people without warrant. He can restrict the right of assembly and expel people who are considered political extremists.

The policies are restrictive. But the Chilean government claims that this is the best way to make the country stable again after so many years of turmoil. According to Pinochet, these measures will prevent left-wing extremists from gaining inroads into the government again.

When Pinochet took over, the inflation rate in Chile was over

*General Augusto Pinochet Ugarte,
president of Chile*

500 percent. It has since dropped. However, Chile owes a lot of money to other countries and there is still much unemployment. There is a housing shortage and the need for improved public works and education.

By the mid-1980s, cracks appeared in the tough facade of Pinochet's government. Laborers, farmers, and professional groups demanded an end to military rule. They recalled the days from the 1890s to the 1970s, when Chile had the reputation as being one of the most democratic countries in the Americas. Vigorous young activists were arrested. Among those were Rodolfo Seguel, the leader of the Copper Workers Confederation, the largest labor union in Chile. Many people were killed and injured in riots and confrontations with police and the military that continued through 1984. As the disturbances continued, church leaders remained outspoken, urging the government to loosen its political reins.

Yet today, Pinochet seems able to stay in power despite growing opposition. But who knows what changes the future will bring to the people of this fascinating, cosmopolitan country?

Marble steps lead to the top of Santiago's Santa Lucía Park.

Chapter 5

LAND OF EXCITING

CONTRASTS

There are palm trees, benches, and hundreds of street vendors selling everything from shoes to fruit ringing the foot of Santiago's Santa Lucía Park. This is the hill where Pedro de Valdivia built his fort in February, 1541. Marble staircases now lead to the top; from there you can see the buildings of the Catholic University across the street. Three hundred years ago, only wooden stake fences and adobe mud protected the tiny garrison from attack. Once Valdivia's girl friend, Inés de Suárez, had to command the conquistadors when the Mapuche attacked the fort while the general was away.

The hill has seen a lot since it was born amid the growlings and rumblings of Chile's geological birth eons ago. The Indians had dedicated it to the god of pain. It was a fitting title considering the centuries of bloodshed that followed the arrival of the Spanish. In more peaceful days, Bernardo O'Higgins attempted to build an observatory on its peak but the effort failed. For a time, the hill was ignored. It was used as a garbage dump for years. But a local citizen, Don Benjamín Vicuña Mackenna, looked at the hill, wishing it were a park.

He convinced the city to do something with Santa Lucía Hill because of its important role in Chilean history. The town fathers

Santa Lucía Park is a favorite spot for recreation and relaxation.

finally agreed to his plans and allowed him to use prisoners to
help construct a park. From 1872 to 1874, Vicuña Mackenna
directed the work of the convicts. They carried up all the soil that
now covers the hill on their backs! They planted trees and shrubs
and transformed a dump into one of the most beautiful parks in
Chile. On its ridge is the Castillo Gonzalez, a castle with ramparts
that overlook Avenida Bernardo O'Higgins, Santiago's main street
(nicknamed The Alameda). Another building, the Castillo
Hidalgo, now houses the Popular Arts Museum in what were
once prison cells.

On Sundays, young Chileans like to stroll along Santa Lucía
Hill. The boys and girls laughingly call their hand-in-hand walks
amor al aire libre (or "love in the open air").

The hill has become the center of life in Santiago, a city of about
four million. But another peak is also important. Anchoring the
edge of town is the 945-foot-high (288 meter) San Cristobal Hill. It
is topped with a statue of the Virgin Mary, a gift from France. At
night, the statue is lighted and can be seen for miles. You can

Statue of the Virgin Mary atop San Cristobal Hill (left).
A cable car affords a scenic trip to the hilltop (right).

walk to the top of San Cristobal, drive a car up, or even take a cable car. A terrace is at the top, with a small cafe that has great desserts. You can sit high above the city smog on the restaurant patio and watch all of Santiago bustle far below.

The Santiago zoo is about one third of the way up the hill and has a great display of Chile's native animals and birds.

Santiago is Chile's capital. Many government buildings line the streets and the main squares. La Moneda, the presidential palace, was built in 1805. One plaza in front of the palace is used for the changing of the presidential guard, which is a colorful pageant. This palace can also be used as a shortcut! Since La Moneda takes up a whole city block, busy Chileans can cut through a patio that connects its two main entrances. That way, no one has to walk around the sprawling old building.

The palace was bombed when the junta staged its coup in 1973. But it was repaired in time for President Pinochet's inauguration in 1981. Some of the surrounding offices still have bullet marks from those terrible days.

The Hotel Carrera is on one side of the square near the palace. This has a famous rooftop restaurant with a removable dance floor over the swimming pool.

Chile is a Catholic country and Santiago is a city of Catholic churches. Many are very ancient. Do you think Santo Domingo is old? It was dedicated in 1771. But the national cathedral is even older. It was built in 1558 and contains many relics, or memorials of saints. The objects used in celebrating the Catholic Mass ceremony there are very valuable. They are made of solid silver and decorated with rubies and emeralds.

Workers started building Santiago's Church of San Francisco in 1568 and finally completed the job in 1618. For ten pesos, you can tour the church and see all the paintings and statues.

But Santiago is also very modern. One of its subway lines travels directly under The Alameda. The trains are very fast and clean. Each stop is color coded to help people who cannot read the station signs. By knowing the proper color, riders can get off at the right stop. The subway fare is only about twenty cents in American money.

Staying in touch with its past, Santiago has sixteen major museums, or *museos*. But a *museo* in Chile might also be an art gallery. The museums contain the usual historical artifacts as well as paintings and sculpture. An aviation museum and an antique car museum are also located in Santiago and are popular with young people.

Chile is a very international country, and Santiago reflects this in its restaurants. Some of the more famous restaurants are: Da Carla (Italian), Lung Fung (Chinese), Munchen (German), La Cascade (French), and Coco Loco (seafood). Can you guess what the Drive-In Charles serves?

Santiago landmarks: The presidential palace,
La Moneda (top); Santiago's modern subway (above);
Santiago's cathedral (left), across from Plaza de Armas

More than 3,800,000 people live in Santiago (above).
The Alameda (below) is Santiago's beautiful main thoroughfare.

Arts and leisure in Santiago: Fine Arts Museum (left); enjoying ice cream cones (right)

Of course, there are also dozens of Chilean restaurants, many of which have musical entertainment as well. Strolling minstrels serenade customers at lunch in the Adobes de Argomedo. Folklore shows can be seen at El Canta Gallo, El Pollo Dorado, and many others.

Nestled between the modern high-rise buildings are the marketplaces where shoppers can buy food and souvenirs. One of the busiest is on Recoleta Street. All of Chile congregates here to buy and sell handcrafted items, ranging from dolls to saddles.

Santiago is a typical big city, full of noise and traffic, with wealthy suburbs, neat middle class housing, and crowded slums. It is a city where everyone walks downtown at night, visiting the clubs, watching the other strollers, buying ice cream, and meeting friends. On clear days, when the air pollution is not too bad, you can see the Andes. Ski resorts on the slopes of the mountains can be reached in about an hour's drive to the east. An hour to the west is the beach. Chileans say that one of the nicest things about Santiago is that it is so easy to get away from when a vacation is needed.

Valparaíso's waterfront (facing page) and its twisting side streets (above) attract tourists.

When Chileans talk about vacations, they mention two major
locales. First, there's the Viña del Mar-Valparaíso area, just 74
miles (119 kilometers) west of the capital. Chileans call Valparaíso
"Pancho" or "El Puerto." American Peace Corps workers there in
the 1960s nicknamed it "Valpo." Secondly, there's the lake
country around Puerto Montt, 661 miles (1,064 kilometers) south
of Santiago. Let's visit "Valpo" first. This is Chile's major port,
and a huge naval installation stands at the edge of town.

Valparaíso is divided into two parts. The lower section is called
"The Basin." It hugs the rim of the sea. Many twisting streets
wander through this old section of the city, which is famous as a
leave station for sailors from around the world who are in port.
The other part of town is sprinkled along the hills, with their
colorful mixture of mansions and hovels.

This city is noted for its Arturo Prat Naval School, the Beaux
Arts Museum, the Catholic University, and branches of the
University of Chile and a major technical university. Many of
Chile's famous writers and poets have lived here.

The resort town of Viña del Mar

The beaches in Valparaíso are nice. But if you want really great sand to build ocean-side castles, try Viña del Mar, about ten minutes up the coast. This elegant town, full of gardens and flowers, is nicknamed "The Pearl of the Pacific." It has been a tradition to come here to get away from the bustle of the everyday world. Vacationers stay in the guest houses, eat in the seafood restaurants, send postcards home, take rides in the horse drawn carriages, and generally relax. Between Viña and Valparaíso, as in many spots along the coast, you can watch fisherman beaching their boats and cleaning their catch. Eventually, some of those fish might be in your evening soup.

Clockwise from top:
Viña del Mar's rugged coastline;
fishing village near Valparaíso;
cleaning the catch in Angelmo

Puerto Montt waterfront (left) and a church built in the German style (right)

Now let's travel to Puerto Montt in south central Chile. Puerto Montt is the capital of the Lake District. Fishing fans from miles around come here to try their luck in catching brown or rainbow trout. The countryside around the city looks like Bavaria or Switzerland, a reason why many settlers from those Old World areas came here. The Germans first arrived in 1852 and still make up a significant portion of the 85,000 persons who live in Puerto Montt. Some of the chalets in the surrounding hills could be straight from a picture book about Europe. Artists enjoy coming here to paint in the harbor area.

German farmers in nearby Osorno eventually made that town one of the centers of agricultural production in Chile.

Between Puerto Montt and Osorno are vast lakes, volcanoes, and parks. The Petrohué Falls 53 miles (85 kilometers) east of Puerto Montt are among the most photographed anywhere. The

Lava boulders (left) lining Petrohué Falls, east of Puerto Montt. The beach at Arica (right)

cold, blue-green waters roar out of the mountains here like champagne from a bottle.

Now that we've looked at central Chile and several of the country's major cities, let's visit some of the towns in the north. The Chileans call this region "The Great North." Although much of the land is desert, many people—mostly miners—live here. The large coastal cities of Arica, Iquique, Antofagasta, and La Serena are modern and bustling. Their beaches are perfect for sunbathers and vacationers from elsewhere in South America who are just discovering the beaches along the coast here.

Do you feel adventurous today? Would you like to take a horseback ride across the desert and camp at night? A lot of young students are doing that now so they can closely study the desert. Of course, they have guides who help them get from one oasis to another. A trip alone in this arid land is certainly not recommended! Remember the Men of Chile.

Indian ruins near San Pedro de Atacama

One of the tiniest villages in the north is San Pedro de Atacama. Only 892 people live there. It was once very remote, isolated by the stretches of sand and rock. But today a highway links the town to Antofagasta, a city of more than 162,000 people. Yet the road hasn't made that much difference. Times do not change quickly in the desert.

Centuries ago, Indians lived near the springs in San Pedro de Atacama. Thousands of their ancient graves have been discovered. Father Gustave Le Paige, a Belgian priest and archaeologist who made this tiny town his home, knew a lot about the region. He opened a museum to display the artifacts he found. Room after room is filled with Indian mummies. Some have their original hair still intact because the desert where they were buried was so dry. You will learn a lot about these ancient people by talking with the museum curators.

Left: Volcanic geysers at Tatio. Right: Andean condor

Not far from San Pedro de Atacama are the volcanic geysers of Tatio, which erupt every morning around dawn. Also nearby is Chiu Chiu, the site of an old Indian fortress. The many carvings on the rocks in the neighborhood were made a thousand years ago.

Now let us travel to southern Chile, where you will see an entirely different landscape. This land is the end of the world. That's how some of the first settlers described this frosty one third of Chile. The region is punctuated only by a few roads, some Indian villages, and several fishing communities. Flying over the region is awesome. For hours, all you will see are mountains, volcanoes, bays, lakes, snowfields, and glaciers. Sometimes you can even see a condor, that huge bird of the Andes, swiftly flying so high it seems to be able to outrace your airplane.

The world's southernmost city is here. Punta Arenas was founded and opened to colonists in 1874. About 79,000 people live

Statue of Ferdinand Magellan (left), gazing toward the Strait of Magellan. Punta Arenas business district (right)

here. In the Plaza de Armas is a tall statue of Magellan, whose ships first sailed through the strait and around the tip of South America. It is supposed to be good luck to kiss the foot of the statue. No one is sure that this works, but it is a lot of fun.

Punta Arenas used to be the headquarters for seal hunters and whalers. It therefore has a long tradition of being a sailor's town. But now, the main sources of income come from sheep and livestock herds on surrounding farms, from oil wells, and from king crab fisheries offshore. Punta Arenas is the jumping-off point for excursions to Cape Horn and the many glaciers to the south.

Paine National Park

The Towers of Paine, a saw-toothed mountain ridge, are popular tourist sights, as is Milodon Cave. Many giant, prehistoric fossils have been found in this cave. You can even see flocks of rheas (which resemble ostriches) and herds of deer on your drive to the Towers and the cave. Sometimes, you might even be able to spot a red fox hiding in the rocks near the narrow highway.

Chile's Antarctic can be reached by ship or by small plane. Its territory on this continent is called Land of O'Higgins. But this snowbound land is not empty! Chilean naturalists have discovered thirty-two varieties of birds living in Antarctica. Many species of fish and marine animals live in the sea.

Here, where the land ends, visitors can truly appreciate what an amazing and diverse country Chile is.

Heavy industry thrives in the Concepción area.
Huachipato steel plant (above) and the petroleum refinery (below)
process Chile's raw materials for sale.

Chapter 6

CHILE'S ECONOMIC TREASURES

Chile is sometimes called the "Shoestring Nation" because of its long thin shape. But that does not mean that Chile's natural resources exist "only by a shoestring." Certainly not! The country supplies much of the world's copper and other minerals. It also grows very fine agricultural products. Fishing is important, too.

Mines are located all over the country. In the Norte Grande, from Arica to Copiapó, copper, nitrate, iron, sulfur, gold, silver, and quartz are mined. A fine white clay, called kaolin, has also been discovered in this region. The kaolin is used in making porcelain, textiles, and paper. Deposits of molybdenum, a brittle, lustrous metallic element, are being tapped for making electrical components and points for spark plugs. Also, large deposits of lithium offer great expectations for mining in the future.

In the mountainous region called Norte Chico (Little North), from Copiapó to La Ligua, more copper has been found, as well as iron, gold, silver, and mercury. The ore is hauled from the mines to the two large ports of Huasco and Chañaral where it is loaded on ships.

The central area from the Aconcagua River to the Bío-Bío is basically agricultural. However, miners there have found copper, gold, silver, limestone, quartz, slate, kaolin, and pozzuolana — volcanic ash used in making cement. A very soft mineral called talc, used for making talcum powder and lubricants, is mined as well. Coal has been discovered farther south between the Bío-Bío River and the Lastarria mountain range.

Iron, lead, and oil are found as you continue on down the shoestring country. In the channel area, at the tip of Chile, more than 12.6 million barrels of oil are produced a year.

It is estimated that Chile sits atop the world's greatest reserves of copper, figured at more than 130 billion tons! Its reserves of iron ore might be as high as a billion tons!

For a long time, the mines were owned by foreign companies, usually from the United States. In the 1950s, the Chilean Congress considered nationalizing, or taking over, the mines. But it wasn't until July 11, 1971, that a constitutional amendment finally approved the move. Control of the mines is now in the hands of the Chilean National Copper Corporation (CODELCO-CHILE), which acts as the government's representative. But dependence on copper mining had made Chile's economy rather one-sided. In 1976, copper represented 60 percent of all exports. Currently, it represents only about 45 percent. But any drop in the world market price for copper can really hurt the economy. So the country is experimenting with other mining and industrial projects.

President Allende's socialist government nationalized about five hundred industries when it was in power. But the junta has subsequently returned most of them to private owners. More than a million people now work for companies that produce textiles,

Sawmill near Skyring, north of Punta Arenas

glass, tires, timber products, leather, locomotives, autos, tractors, and many other important items.

Much of Chile's recent economic growth is supervised by the Corporacion de Fomento, the Development Corporation, and its subsidiaries such as the National Petroleum Enterprise and the Pacific Steel Company. These corporations accept foreign investment but are owned in part by the government.

Chile still has a strong agricultural base. When the conquistadors arrived, they found the Indians using irrigation systems and growing plants they had never seen in Europe. Among these products was the potato.

The Indians would store the potato for the winter by making *chuno*, or potato flour. Corn, sweet potatoes, squash, kidney and green beans, cucumbers, papayas, avocados, and prickly pears were also grown in those ancient days.

Harvesting grapes at the Concha y Toro winery near Santiago

The Spaniards thought all these crops tasted pretty good, so they continued raising them. They also grew wheat on the haciendas and cultivated grapes along the mountain slopes. As you remember, the land was concentrated in the hands of only a few people for centuries. Those who did not own any land worked for the rich "patrón" on the hacienda.

The tenant workers at the haciendas were called *inquilinos*. They had to get their food, houses, and protection from the patrón. The patrón could even tell them how to vote. But as we mentioned, land ownership in Chile has gone through many changes. The land was also worked by migrant workers, sharecroppers, and small and medium-sized landowners.

During the administration of President Jorge Alessandri (1958-1964), the first Agrarian Reform Law was enacted. Under this law, the government sold or gave away some of the property it owned.

Hillside and small farm near Puerto Aisén

Throughout President Eduardo Frei's government (1964-1970), a large number of private farms were made into cooperatives called *asentamientos*. Much of the land was taken from haciendas that were larger than 200 acres (81 hectares). At the end of three to five years, the program participants were to vote. They were to decide then if they wanted to remain in a cooperative or divide the property among themselves.

Salvador Allende's government (1970-1973) continued to apply the same law and expanded it. Most Chilean land eventually became state owned. Allende tried to broaden the principle of the *asentamientos* by establishing Agrarian Reform Centers. More peasants were qualified to join these cooperatives than the earlier ones. The centers were popular among some peasants but not among others.

A few felt the reforms were going too fast, but others felt they weren't moving fast enough. Several left-wing groups even seized the property of medium-sized landowners and established their own communes.

Ranch along the Estuario Relanclavi

The landowners complained to the government. But the Allende regime did not have enough control in the countryside to put a stop to the unrest. People were very afraid. The military junta took advantage of the disturbances, attracting supporters who opposed the land reform program.

The military rulers decided to make some changes in the system when they took over. Peasants were again allowed to own their own land, instead of having to belong to a cooperative. By November of 1976, more than 25,000 titles of land had been issued to people who previously did not have any property. However, most Chileans were not able to participate in the new land purchase programs. At least 350,000 families did not qualify under the terms of the junta's laws.

Under the present-day laws, property can now be sold. Many of the peasants who did get land when the junta came into power

An asentamiento, *or cooperative farm, near Curicó*

had to resell their property. They were not able to get enough credit to buy seed and livestock. The big, wealthy landowners began buying up this land again. So the Chilean government is still trying to find a fair way for poor citizens to get and keep their land.

In 1978, the government started a program to train peasants who became new landowners. These people now learn how to rotate crops, use fertilizer, and better manage their farms.

Citrus fruit, wheat, oats, corn, rice, barley, rye, beans, peas, potatoes, flax, hemp, and sunflowers are major crops. Many grapes are cultivated for making wine. Did you know that France (which is famous for its own wine) buys more delicious Chilean wine than any other country?

Agriculture is very limited in the far north. Crops can only be grown in the little oases found in the desert ravines. Some citrus

Huasos rounding up cattle

fruits that flourish in warm weather can be cultivated here, much as in the states of Florida and Texas. Papayas, apricots, peaches, and custard apples from the north taste exceptionally good. Pisco, a powerful brandy, is made from the desert-grown grapes.

The central zone can grow a greater variety of farm products. The soil here is rich and deep, sometimes going down several hundred feet. Watermelons, tangerines, almonds, walnuts, tobacco, cherries, wheat, peas, beans, and numerous other crops can easily be cultivated.

South of the Bío-Bío River, extensive grasslands carpet the countryside. You will see large herds of cattle munching contentedly. They also like the clover that grows well in southern Chile.

Huasos, the Chilean cowboys, are a common sight racing after cattle during roundup time. The huasos wear wide-brimmed flat hats that will not blow off easily. Another part of their "uniforms" are *mantas*, short ponchos that do not tangle in their riding gear as a long coat might. It is said that the mantas were developed by Indians after they captured horses from the Spaniards.

*An abundance of fresh seafoods, such as king crabs (right),
fill a seafood stand at a Santiago market (left).*

Raising beets is less glamorous than galloping around the range
all day, but this product is also very important for the economy of
southern Chile. Many people here work in the lumber camps and
mills as well. Because the altitude suppresses disease-causing
organisms, the forests are free from many diseases that affect trees
in other places. Chilean timber products are therefore highly
regarded. In the extreme south, millions of sheep are raised on the
vast meadows and uplands. Their thick wool coats help them stay
warm in this rugged land!

Despite the increased farm output, Chile still has to import
some food. In 1973, the country imported $700 million worth of
items. Currently, the figure has been lowered to around $200
million. Eventually, Chile would like to be fairly self-sufficient.
The people then would not need to buy food produced in other
nations.

The sea provides an abundance of treasures for the Chileans.
Seaweed is used in fertilizers, as an ingredient in ice cream, and

for a dozen other food products. Fishing is a major activity for Chileans who live along the coast.

Can you guess what varieties of seafoods are available? Here are some from the waters off the coast of northern Chile: bonito, tuna, swordfish, anchovy, sardine, sawfish, sole, and smelt, and exotic species such as jurel, lisa, robalo, corvina, hake, red and black conger eel, octopus, abalone, limpet, clam, tacas, crab, and mussels. Off central Chile, one can catch prawns and lobsters as well.

Seafood products are sold canned or ground into meal, as well as frozen, dried, salted, or smoked. The principal fish-processing plants and ports for the fishing fleets are located in Arica, Iquique, Tocopilla, Mejillones, Antofagasta, Caldera, Coquimbo, Valparaíso, San Antonio, Talcahuano, Valdivia, Puerto Montt, Calbuco, Ancud, Quellón, and Punta Arenas.

Chilean industry makes many products, ranging from yeast to automobiles, tires, and furniture.

Chile takes very good care of its workers. In 1925, a compulsory sickness and accident insurance plan was established. Medical costs, and even some burial expenses, are usually covered. The labor unions appreciate this system, which grew out of the labor unrest in Chile after World War I.

A new social security program went into effect in 1981, managed by private organizations under governmental guidelines. The system no longer relies on heavy contributions from the workers. It is an individual savings plan, in which more than 1.3 million workers were participating by 1982.

There are approximately 3,340,000 full-time workers in the country. However, 26 percent of the population was still unemployed during the mid-1980s.

The copper miners are the highest paid of all the laboring class.

They have pleasant homes with many modern conveniences. However, there are many poor people who flock to the major cities seeking work.

The poor are almost "lost people" because there is often a scarcity of jobs and great numbers of these people have no work. Every large Chilean city is fringed with slums. This is a serious problem which the government is attempting to correct.

CEMA-Chile is a private foundation that assists poorer women in many ways. More than two million women participate in CEMA-Chile programs that range from promoting craft work for sale to teaching hygiene and baby care.

There are more than 9,756 centers throughout the country where the women come for classes. CEMA-Chile teachers work for many organizations. Among them are the Chilean Red Cross, Laborer-Farm Worker Department of the Catholic University, the Association for the Protection of the Family, and the Department of Social Advancement of the University of Chile. The foundation is supported by the sale of its craft goods in 350 artisan shops. The women produce beautiful weavings, pottery, paintings, dolls, jewelry, and other artifacts.

CEMA-Chile is also assisted by donations and contributions from the Polla Chilena de Beneficencia (one of the two lotteries in Chile), from one day's proceeds at the Santiago and Valparaíso racetracks, and by a tax on movie tickets. Because of the work by CEMA-Chile, more women are becoming self-sufficient and are able to increase their family income.

For a long time, it was hard for Chileans to visit another country. The mountains, deserts, and seas made it almost impossible to come and go. However, air travel has made a big difference. Now it is easy to cross the Andes Mountains.

The Chilean Andes, as seen from an airplane, are magnificent.

A stretch of the Pan-American Highway crosses the Atacama Desert.

The view of the sun rising over the snow-covered Andes far below is a beautiful sight from an airplane. The national airline is Lan Chile. It flies to many international airports around the world, including the United States.

There are about 30,000 miles (48,000 kilometers) of roads in Chile, the best of which are in the central part of the country. However, most towns, even in the desert, are connected to the outside world by at least one good road.

The Inter-American Highway runs from Arica south to Llay-Llay. From there one branch crosses the Andes at La Cumbre Pass to Argentina. The other branch continues on to Santiago. Another primary international highway in the Lake District connects Osorno to Argentina via the Puyehue Pass. The longest national highway connects Arica in the north to Puerto Montt in the south. It is part of the Pan-American Highway that starts in Alaska and ends in Chile.

Gaily-painted steam locomotive (left). A typical Chilean household (right)

Chile was the first South American country to build an electric railroad. The line connected Santiago and Valparaíso. There are thousands of miles of good rail lines in the country, most of which are owned by the government. Five international railways connect Chile with its neighbors. Passenger trains run to Peru, Bolivia, and Argentina. Taking a train across the mountains can be a scary but spectacular journey.

But not everyone wants to travel. Chileans enjoy life at home. Television is popular. Many people have at least one set. The regular stations carry musical and variety programs, reruns from Europe and the United States, and news shows. The Catholic and National universities also have stations that offer good programs.

Just about everyone, from the miners to the sheepherders, has a radio. That is their link with the outside world. A couple of stations in the capital carry classical music, but rock and roll and country-western music from the United States are more popular.

It can be a big surprise to turn on your hotel room radio in Santiago and have every station playing the latest English-language pop tune.

There are dozens of magazines and newspapers in Chile. Youngsters enjoy reading Spanish translations of classics such as *Moby Dick*. But comic books are best, according to many young people. Favorite characters are El Ratón Miguelito and Pepita. Who are they? Those are the Chilean names for Mickey Mouse and Blondie!

El Mercurio is the country's oldest newspaper. It was started more than 150 years ago in Valparaíso and is now published in Santiago. It acts as the country's official voice and is full of government news. But during soccer tournaments, nobody thinks about politics. Everyone reads the paper just for the sports.

To run all the devices that make life pleasant and easy—from radio stations to printing presses to industrial machinery—Chile depends heavily on its natural water resources. Waterfalls throughout the country are used to produce power. In fact, one of the largest hydroelectric plants in South America is located in Chile. It opened in 1968. Another huge hydroelectric project was started in 1981 at Colbun-Machicura-Chiburgo. The facility should be fully operating by 1990.

In the desert north, experiments are being conducted with solar power. The Chileans see no reason for all that good energy from the sun to go to waste.

So from the wet to the hot and everything in between, the Chileans are using whatever natural resources they can to make their country prosper.

Villager in the Atacama region (above left); Chilean father and daughter (above right);
two girls of Puerto Montt (below left); and a huaso wearing his manta (below right)

Chapter 7

LAND OF POETS

Chile is lucky. It can draw upon dozens of ethnic backgrounds as a base for its own culture, its personal viewpoint toward life. We saw how the Chilean people evolved from the mingling of the Spanish conquistadors and the Indians. The waves of immigrants also added a bit of themselves to the Chilean whole: Germans, English, Czechs, Yugoslavs, Arabs, Italians, Orientals, and many others. It makes for a fascinating mixture, tied together by the Spanish language and three hundred years of tradition.

Chile is probably one of the most European of all the South American nations. There are only a few hundred thousand Indians remaining with a pure bloodline. So the new arrivals from all over the world have made a strong impression on Chile.

This bubbling stew is perfect material for writers. Poets and philosophers seem to grow naturally from the Chilean soil. The land with all its variety and excitement shapes the people in all their diversity. The Chileans in turn reflect on who they are and where they are going. This is what we mean by culture—the shaping of ideas.

Mapuche women pose in front of their home.

As in many South American countries, cultural expression—whether in painting, sculpture, essays, or poems—is closely tied to political statement. The history of revolution in this part of the world might very well affect how artists and writers portray their subjects. The people of Chile had to fight to gain independence. Often, they had to continue the battle against dictators who took over after the Spaniards were driven out.

At first, the Spaniards did everything they could to destroy the Indian way of life. In the early days of colonization, they were interested only in acquiring treasures. However, one conquistador named Alonso de Ercilla y Zúñiga was a poet as well as a soldier. He marched into Chile with García Hurtado de Mendoza, the son of the viceroy of Peru. Whenever he was not fighting the Mapuche, he rested and wrote poems on scraps of bark or leather. It was hard to get paper on the Chilean frontier! Through his eyes, we can get a good view of what the 1560s were like. His major work is called *La Araucana,* which was his name for the Mapuche. The name comes from the words for "water" and "clay." The Spaniards always called the Mapuche the "people of the muddy water" because they usually lived near rivers.

Chile's beloved Gabriela Mistral, affectionately called "The Divine Gabriela," was South America's first Nobel Prize-winning author.

Ercilla probably didn't mean to glorify the Indians. He just wanted to show the bravery of his fellow soldiers. But today, Chilean schoolchildren can recite most of his entire poem by heart. They then discuss it from the viewpoint of the Mapuche, who were never conquered by the Spaniards.

Chileans are fascinated by their history. One Spanish writer remarked that there was nothing that has not been studied about Chile's past. And it is that past that affects how the Chileans look at their todays . . . and their tomorrows.

The country's greatest literary achievements are in the works of three authors: Gabriela Mistral, Pablo Neruda, and Vicente Huidobro. Every Chilean is proud of what this trio has done for their country. In fact, Mistral won the coveted Nobel Prize in literature in 1945. She was the first South American to win the award for her writings. Neruda won the same international honor in 1971.

Mistral (1889-1957) was the daughter of a rural schoolteacher who understood the difficulty of life in the poor countryside. Although she traveled a great deal, Mistral always wrote about her homeland. In "We Are All Going to Be Queens," she described the little village where she was born. This was in the Elqui valley, "surrounded by a hundred mountains or more." The town in which she grew up was "in the vineyards of Monte Grande, with their pure white bays." She embraced both the old and new worlds of the common people with her words, which made her a favorite of the mestizos. They called her "The Divine Gabriela."

She loved children and often wrote about them. The following verse was directed to the youngsters of the rural schools. Perhaps it was a remembrance of her own youth.

"Little children's feet,/blue from the cold,/How can they see you and not cover you,/Dear God!"

Pablo Neruda (1904-1973) enjoyed long walks in the countryside. He would always wear the poncholike manta as would the huasos, the cowboys. These hikes would help him collect his thoughts. When receiving the Nobel Prize he said, "I come from an unknown province, from a country separated from the rest by a rugged geography. I was the most forlorn of the poets and my poetry was regional, sorrowful, and full of rain. But I always had confidence in man. I never lost hope."

Neruda's real name was Neftalí Ricardo Reyes, but he probably changed his name to protect his identity because of his leftist political leanings.

Neruda was born in the south of Chile. His mother died when he was very young; his father was a laborer. "I come from the people and/I sing for the people. . .," he wrote in his epic poem "Cancion de Gesta."

He remembered his childhood and was never afraid to talk about his humble beginnings. Once, he told how his father dreamed of buying a piano for the family. But he was never able to afford one. So Neruda often said that the only piano notes he heard when he was growing up were the sounds of raindrops when they seeped through the roof. They would splash into the pots and pans placed throughout the house to protect the floor.

As with many young Chilean poets, he was influenced by The Divine Gabriela. She was the principal of a girls' school when they first met. She shared many books with him and encouraged him to write.

Neruda became a journalist and eventually entered the diplomatic service. Among other high-ranking positions, he was Chile's ambassador to France. Despite all this traveling, he continued writing his poems and plays. His works eventually grew from purely personal reflections to condemnations of injustice where he saw hunger, poverty, and oppression. In "The Blind Man with a Tambourine," he described the life of a beggar. In "Neighborhood without Light," he talked about the squalid aspects of a city and how the poverty affects people. His "Workshops at Night" complained about grim working conditions in factories.

It was no wonder the poor people of his country loved him so much. They knew he could understand their feelings.

Vicente Huidobro (1893-1948) was another poet widely admired by the Chileans. Unlike the other two poets, Huidobro was descended from Chilean aristocrats. One of his grandfathers founded the Conservative party.

Huidobro started a movement called "creationism." He believed that the artist should not imitate what was seen in life. Instead, he said, the poet (or artist, musician, or sculptor) should make something that could not exist apart from the artist. He would not say "the bird nests on a branch," but rather "the bird nests on a rainbow."

Huidobro was very funny. Children loved his works because he would often arrange his poems in various shapes on the page. If he was writing about a church, the words would be put in the shape of a cross. "If I didn't do at least one crazy thing a year, I'd go crazy," he chuckled.

He was very sensitive. One of his poems, "Serenade of Laughing Life," went like this:

Three hundred sixty-five trees in the forest
Three hundred sixty-five forests in the year
How many does it take to make up a century
A child would get lost in them until the end
    of the century
And would learn all the bird songs

Not everyone liked how Huidobro looked at his world. But he didn't care. He would just laugh and compose in whatever form he wished. Although he lived most of his productive life in Paris, he possessed that independent spirit that is typical of Chileans throughout their history. Other respected writers include Nicanor Parra, Manuel Rojas, Benjamín Subercaseaux, Vicente Pérez Rosales, and Pedro Prado.

Authors are not the only artists who have that vibrant Chilean spirit. Other cultural disciplines captured it as well. Even contemporary painters such as Roberto Matta, Ernesto Barreda, Nemesio Antúnez, and Enrique Zañartu have gone their own way. Respected sculptors include Marta Colvin and Rebecca Matte. Famous musicians—both of them pianists—are Claudio Arrau and Rosita Renard.

Works by composers Domingo Santa Cruz and Enrique Soro are widely respected throughout the world. Another composer, Carlos Isamitt, specialized in music with an Indian theme.

Works of many Chilean artists enhance public places.
This mural graces the Universidad de Concepción theater.

Intellectuals and students in Chile have often been the leaders
of the reform movements in their country. Such important leaders
as Presidents Eduardo Frei and Salvador Allende became
interested in politics when they attended the university. Frei, for
instance, organized seminars on social justice when he was in
school. He later went to Paris and studied under Jacques Maritain,
a leader in the French Christian Democrat movement. Frei also
admired the encyclicals, or letters, written on social issues by
Catholic Popes Leo XIII, Pius XI, and John XXIII. Many of
Allende's principal advisers were university professors.

Chile's rich ethnic heritage is reflected in this group of schoolchildren.

Chileans are among the most literate of any people in South America. This factor contributes to their interest in how the country functions. Their country was the first Latin American nation to set up a public education system, which was organized in 1842. The Catholic church ran the schools in colonial days, and the coming of independence meant a learning explosion. By now, almost everyone, even the poorest person, can read and write at least a little bit.

Young people in Chile must attend school through the eighth grade. School is free and runs from March through December, the winter months in this part of the world. There are nursery schools for youngsters up to five years old. Then they must go to elementary school. When they are fifteen, the young people can move on to four years of high school. There they take arts and science in college preparatory classes or vocational training courses. University schooling lasts from four to six years.

Universidad de Chile is state supported and has more than 22,000 students.

The names of the Chilean universities, in Spanish, are: Universidad de Chile, Universidad Catolica de Chile, Universidad de Concepción, Universidad Tecnica Federico Santa Maria, Universidad Catolica de Valparaíso, Universidad de Santiago, Universidad Austral de Chile, and Universidad del Norte. The Universidad de Concepción is the only nongovernment and non-church related university in Latin America, which makes it a real exception to the rule.

Students in Chile have to be at school by 8 A.M. Boys and girls usually have from three to four hours of instruction in the morning, with ten-minute breaks between each class. After the long morning session, everyone goes home for lunch and enjoys a rest period called a siesta. Two or three hours later, they do their homework. Some stay at school doing sports or extra activities.

But in some crowded schools, especially in the *callampas* around the big cities, students can only attend half days. A *callampa*

Chilean high school girls in uniform.
Futbol, or soccer (right), is Chile's most popular sport.

(which means "mushroom") is the nickname given to a
shantytown that springs up around a city almost overnight—just
like mushrooms.

Most children walk to school or take city buses. Sometimes they
are very loud and rowdy on the buses. Therefore, many drivers do
not like to have students aboard. Besides, the students travel for a
reduced fare. Since the bus drivers work on commission, they do
not make as much money when the youngsters ride.

Students in lower grades study Spanish, mathematics, natural
and social science, art, handicrafts, physical education, and
religion. A foreign language is introduced by the time students get
to seventh grade. Favorites are English and French. German is
popular in the south. Do you remember why? It is because of all
the German influence in that region, of course. Despite the
government's efforts only 30 percent of the students have a chance
to go to high school.

At a liceo, or high school, students take music lessons and
receive more training in courses started in their earlier grades.
Final exams mean a great deal. If a young person is not doing

well, he or she often has to leave school and find a job. Less than 2 percent of the students graduate from high school.

Sports are very important to all Chileans. There is fierce competition on all levels between schools. In Santiago, everyone's attention focuses on the *futbol* (soccer) games played between University of Chile and the Catholic University. They are traditional rivals and the matches are fought hard. The entire city shuts down and sits in front of television sets to watch. However, swimming, field hockey, basketball, gymnastics, boxing, and volleyball are other popular sports. Chilean tennis players are also very good and are the source of much pride.

Today's Chilean students are not allowed to be as political as they used to be. Many were very involved in left-wing causes at one time. But the conservative junta now in power frowns on political activity. It keeps a close watch on what the students do.

Yet Chile cannot escape its long tradition of a love of learning, of fierce patriotism and pride in being free. Those attitudes will never die in this land of poets.

Music and singing are part of every party.
Traditional songs and folk dances (below) are taught
to the young to keep Chile's heritage alive.

Chapter 8

CHILE OF THE CUECA

Chileans love parties. Whenever several people get together, they enjoy dancing. The *cueca* is the national folk dance of Chile. It is a wild, footstamping type of dance, with plenty of spirit. Most researchers think the cueca did not originate in Chile. Some think it came from Spain because it resembles the flamboyant folk dancing of that country. Others say it came from Africa. But many believe the dance derived from the *zamacueca* of Peru, coming to Chile around 1824.

The dance took on different characteristics depending on the region in which it took root. The cueca is usually accompanied by fast and furious guitar music. Sometimes the harp, accordion, piano, and tambourine are also used. In the north, the guitar is often replaced by a brass or reed band. Everybody watching keeps time by clapping.

You do not need any special clothes to dance the cueca. But strong boots help. Professional dancers usually wear the traditional huaso clothing, complete with boots and jingling spurs.

In the cueca, each partner holds a handkerchief that swirls and twirls over their heads. Dancing the cueca is popular at harvest time, rodeos, Independence Day celebrations, or any other time Chileans gather. They drink wine or pisco, often flavored with sour mix and whipped egg whites, and have a great time to the tune of "Sáquense Los Sombreros." There is even a dance about Antarctica called "La Cueca Blanca"!

Of course, the Chileans do not spend all their time having parties. But they certainly do like to socialize. A boy might take a date to Mass, much as he would to a movie. Going to church is often viewed as a chance to meet and talk to friends. While probably only about 30 percent of the Chileans attend church regularly, they still take their religion seriously.

Indian and Spanish heritages are evident throughout all forms of worship. Catholic religious practices were introduced by the conquistadors. But the ancient beliefs of the Indians influenced many religious ceremonies. For instance, in the north during the celebration of one festival honoring Mary, the Blessed Mother, parishioners dress in costumes suggestive of pagan days. Groups known as *diabladas* wear grotesque masks and come to church to thank her for favors. Then they make *mandas* or promises to Mary that they will be good.

The people of the north also decorate their religious statues with colorful paper flowers. You can see this in the small oasis town of Toconao, which has several statues of Christ that resemble well-known Chileans. At Pica, in another oasis, an altarpiece shows the Last Supper. The statues are life-size, and many of them look like Spanish aristocrats.

In the Little North and around Valparaíso are brotherhoods that call themselves guardians of the Virgin Mary. These societies

"Christ of the Andes," above Uspallata Pass, proclaims peace between Chile and Argentina.

wear special uniforms that resemble those of the conquistadors. For some reason, they call themselves "Chinese." But their practices have nothing to do with the Chinese culture. No one seems to know how the term originated. Dancing is accompanied by the chanting of prayers made up on the spot. These are similar to the *saetas,* or prayers sung in Seville, Spain, during religious festivals. In Chile, they are called "chants of the divinity."

The Virgin is also the patron of the Chilean armed forces. After winning a decisive victory over the Spaniards, O'Higgins promised to build a shrine in her honor on the site at Maipú. However, it wasn't until 1975 that the building was finally completed.

Even in the work world, the Chilean keeps alive a religious spirit. The fishermen dedicate their boats to St. Peter, their patron saint, on his June 29 feast day. A statue of the saint is taken out of the local church, placed in a boat, and rowed around the fishing grounds to ensure a good catch. Many harbors have a statue of St. Peter overlooking the docks.

Along some roads are small shrines, usually put up where someone has been killed in a traffic accident. Anyone passing by can light a candle in memory of the deceased person. Sometimes the candles start fires in nearby fields, but no one dares tamper with the shrines.

These religious practices are not quite as common among the younger Chileans. Other religions are now making inroads into what was once almost exclusively a Catholic country. About 10 percent of the people now attend Pentecostal, Baptist, or Methodist churches. There are some Chileans who are Jehovah's Witnesses and Mormons.

But a "new Catholicism" is growing in Chile. Small, dedicated Christian communities are springing up in the cities and towns. They are more central to people's lives than the old picturesque customs. These groups are very involved in social work. They are doing very important work and will probably continue to do so in the future.

The Chileans love being with friends. Dining out is considered a big experience. Inviting friends for supper means preparing huge meals. Chilean holidays such as Independence Day on September 18 are lots of fun.

Chilean food is delicious. National dishes range from fish to steak. At the top of the list is *empanada*, which is a meat pie shaped like a small turnover. The pie, which contains either beef, chicken, or fish, is baked until the crust hardens. It is eaten with a hearty Chilean red wine.

Bife a lo pobre is a big steak served with fried potatoes and onion. A pair of fried eggs is placed on top of the steak! The *parrillada* is broiled meat fixed over a small grill. A warning: Chilean cooks enjoy using herbs and peppers. An *aji* or pepper

*Savoring curanto,
a delicious
seafood stew,
at Restaurant Polluco
in Puerto Montt*

can be red, white, or green and eaten plain or with salad dressing. One strong pepper is the *cacho de cabra* or "goat's horn."

Curanto is a meal by itself. In central Chile, this stew is served in pots. Fish, shellfish, meat, and all sorts of vegetables are tossed together and cooked.

On Tenglo Island, across the bay from Puerto Montt, curanto is cooked underground in wet sacks placed atop hot stones. After several hours, this "earth oven" is opened and the tasty combination of goodies is eaten.

Chile's seacoast offers a great variety of food that ends up on a family table. You might like *mariscos,* the huge lobsters captured near Juan Fernández Island. Around Punta Arenas, *centollas,* or marine crabs, are delicious.

Young Chileans like sodas, but a favorite holiday drink is *cola de mono* ("monkey's tail"). This is made with aguardiente, a strong local liquor, coffee, milk, sugar, cinnamon, and egg yolk.

Youngsters start drinking wine while they are small. At first, it is mixed with water. But as they grow up, the boys and girls become used to the wine and the water is phased out.

After supper, which is usually between 9:00 and 11:00 P.M. for adults, Chileans often have herb tea. One variety of tea is made from the cedron plant which is grown in many backyards. This tea has a minty taste.

For dessert, there might be *platano en dulce.* This is bananas sprinkled with corn meal, spices, and powdered sugar. The concoction is then baked and served hot.

It is not wise to drink water in Chile that has not been treated to kill bacteria. Harmful bacteria in the food can also make you sick if it is not properly prepared. This is a problem even in the big cities. But most restaurants and homes are very careful, so there is no need to worry too much if you visit.

Chileans often make a big scene when they meet a special friend. There is much hugging and kissing on each cheek. Even when you shake hands with someone, you should pat them on the arm or shoulders at the same time. It gets quite busy when everyone is hugging, sighing, helloing, patting, and kissing. You have to be very fast to keep up!

Unlike other Spanish-speaking Latin Americans, the Chileans seldom says "*adios,*" which means "good-bye." A lot of the younger people say "*chao*" (pronounced "chow"), from the Italian *ciao,* which means "so long." Usually you will hear Chileans say "*hasta luego,*" which means "until the next time," because they hate to leave their pals.

Today's fast world has meant many changes for Chilean young people. Before World War II, a boy would still serenade his girl friend outside her window. He would sing songs and play a guitar. This is seldom, if ever, done any more.

Education is important. In 1928 Chile began its system of free elementary schools.

There are still some traditional practices, however. In some well-to-do aristocratic families, children come to the table after their parents are seated. No one can start eating until the adults begin.

Young people, especially those in the cities, are no different from those in North America or Europe. They like movies, especially westerns and gangster shows. As with other aspects of Chilean life, dating practices have changed over the years. A chaperone is no longer required on a date. This is an older person who keeps a close watch over the boys and girls. Everyone is glad that practice has been done away with.

Street dancers entertain onlookers in Santiago.

In addition to films, Chileans like the theater. The universities are leaders in producing plays, many of which have been written by native playwrights such as Egon Wolf, Jorge Diaz, or Sergio Vodanovic. The Catholic University used to take a tent theater around to the poor neighborhoods of Santiago, but the project had to shut down for lack of money. The university is now seeking ways to continue the project.

The arrival of a one-man band or an organ grinder still excites youngsters in the poorer sections of the big cities. Often a family of musicians will entertain at street corners, thumping on drums and playing trumpets and cymbals. It is quite an occasion when they walk through the streets. It does not take long for a parade to follow and a crowd to gather.

Youngsters also enjoy playing various games. *Palo ensebado* ("the greased pole") originated in Italy, where it was called *cucana.* This game is played with a tall pole, lubricated with soap or grease, which is driven into the ground. Prizes are tied to the

Music students from the Universidad de Chile sing in a Santiago park.

top of the pole and the players have to climb up the slippery mess to win. This is certainly not an easy task, as you can imagine.

Whenever children do not have much to do, they start a game called *rayuela.* This is a coin pitch that originated in Spain. It is played by throwing disks or money at a line drawn on the ground. The person who gets closest to the line wins everything that had been tossed before. Kite flying is popular in the springtime, with public contests adding to the fun.

Since futbol is so popular, youngsters play everywhere—on any open lot, in the parks, in the streets, at school, and with local clubs. In 1962, Chile hosted the World Cup, the major international soccer championship in which the best countries of the world compete. In that year, Chile placed third. The country always fields a highly respected national team, picked from the cream of the local club players. All the boys dream of the day they might be chosen. Chile played in 1974 during the World Cup games in Munich and in the 1982 games in Spain.

Skiing in the Andes

In the 1982 championships, the team was defeated by West Germany and Algeria in the first round of play. Chile then had to drop out of the tournament. Everyone in the country was disappointed but they promised they would do better in the 1986 games in Colombia.

The international skiing center at Portillo has hosted numerous world class downhill events, such as the 1966 world ski championships. Annual competitions are held in Farellones in July and in Villarrica and Antillanca in August. The Andes are so close that a lot of people take their vacations to ski. For some reason, not many Chileans are interested in cross-country skiing.

The people of Chile are warm and friendly,
eager to face new challenges and accept new ideas.

Chile is noted for its fine horseback riders. Army and police teams always do well in the Olympics. In fact, for years, a Chilean rider has held the international high jumping world record. Both men and women compete on horseback at numerous shows around Chile, carrying on that wonderful tradition of the huaso. Horse racing is also popular. The two main events each year are the Derby in Viña del Mar in January and El Ensayo in Santiago during October. People from around the world come to watch the competitions.

You can see that Chile is a busy land. It is in the slow process of change from a tradition-steeped past to a modern, forward-looking nation. Its people are wondering what their future will bring. Whatever comes, they are eagerly hopeful.

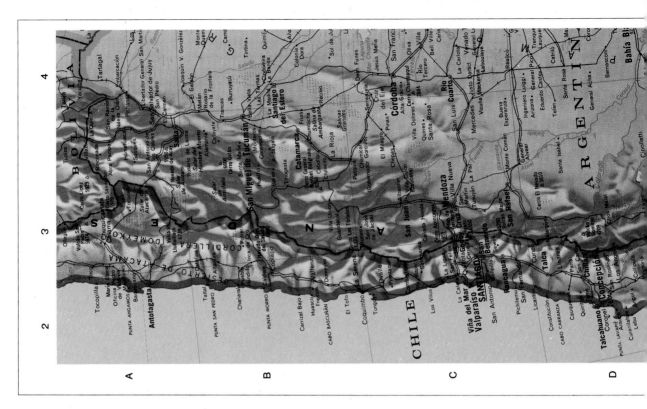

MAP KEY

Altamira	B2	Isla Wellington	F1, 2
Ancud	E2	Isla Wollaston	H3
Antofagasta	A2	Islas Diego Ramírez	H3
Arauco	D2	La Calera	C2
Archipiélago de los Chonos	E, F1, 2	La Ligua	C2
Archipiélago Juan		La Serena	B2
Fernández	C, Pacific Ocean	La Unión	E2
Archipiélago Reina Adelaida	G1, 2	Lago Cochrane	F2
Balmaceda	F2	Lago General Carrera	F2
Baquedano	A2	Lago O'Higgins	F2
Bío-Bío (river)	D2	Lautaro	D2
Cabo Bascuñan	B2	Lebu	D2
Cabo Carranza	D2	Licantén	C, D2
Cabo de Hornos (Cape Horn)	H3	Linares	D2
Calama	A3	Loa	A2, 3
Caldera	B2	Loncoche	D2
Canal de Maraleda	E, F2	Los Ángeles	D2
Cape Horn (Cabo de Hornos)	H3	Los Lagos	D2
Carrizal Bajo	B2	Los Vilos	C2
Castro	E2	Lota	D2
Catalina	B3	María Elena	A3
Cauquenes	D2	Mejillones	A2
Cerro Chato (mountain – 3375)	F2	Melipilla	C2
Cerro San Valentín		Monte Tronador	E2
(mountain – 4058)	F2	Nevado Ojos del Salado	
Cerro Sarmiento		(mountain – 6880)	B2
(mountain – 2300)	G2	Nueva-Imperial	D2
Chañaral	B2	Oficina Pedro de Valdivia	A3
Chile Chico	F2	Ollagüe	A3
Chillán	D2	Osorno	E2
Chuquicamata	A3	Ovalle	C2
Coihaique	F2	Parral	D2
Collipulli	D2	Peninsula Brunswick	G2
Combarbalá	C2	Peninsula de Taitao	F1, 2
Concepción	D2	Pichilemu	C2
Constitución	D2	Porvenir	G2
Copiapó	B2	Potrerillos	B3
Coquimbo	B2	Pueblo Hundido	B2
Cordillera Domeyko	A, B2, 3	Puerto Aisén	F2
Coronel	D2	Puerto Montt	E2
Corral	D2	Puerto Natales	G2
Cunco	D2	Puerto Varas	E2
Curacautin	D2	Punitaqui	C2
Curicó	D2	Punta Angamos	A2

MINI-FACTS AT A GLANCE

GENERAL INFORMATION

Official Name: Republic of Chile

Capital: Santiago

Language: Spanish is the official language. Many Mapuche (Araucanian) Indians use it in addition to their native language. German is the only other significant language, used mainly in the Valdivia region.

Government: At the highest level, Chile is ruled by a president and a *junta*, a group of military officers. They are the heads of the armed forces: army, navy, air force, and militia. The present constitution came into effect in 1981. It provides for direct rule by the junta until 1989, with a phased return after that to full civilian rule by 1997. The junta has dissolved the National Congress and banned all political parties. Military officers now also act as governors of each of the twelve regions and the metropolitan district of Santiago. There are twenty-five provincial subdivisions.

Junta Members: General Augusto Pinochet Ugarte, president; Admiral José Toribio Merino Castro; Air Force Major General Fernando Matthei Aubel; Carabinero General César Mendoza Durán; Army Lieutenant General César Benavides Escobar.

Armed Forces: At the age of twenty, all able-bodied men must receive twelve months of training in the armed forces and serve in the reserves from the ages of twenty-one to forty-five. About 120,000 reach military age each year.

Courts: Judges are still civilians. There are local courts, twelve courts of appeal, and a supreme court. After the 1973 coup, the junta established military tribunals to try its opponents.

Flag: Divided in half horizontally. The upper-left third is blue with a white star. The upper-right two thirds are white. The lower half is red.

National Songs: *"Cancion Nacional de Chile"* (National Anthem of Chile) and *"Dulce Patria"* (Sweet Country)

National Dance: Cueca

National Flower: Copihue (a member of the rose family that grows in central and southern Chile)

Religion: About 80 percent are Roman Catholic; about 5 percent are Jews or Protestants, and some Mapuche Indians still follow their tribal religion.

Money: Peso and centavo (100 centavos to the peso). Currently, coins are for 1, 5, 10, and 50 pesos. Paper bills are for 100, 500, 1,000, and 5,000 pesos.

Weights and Measures: Chile uses the metric system; however, the *quintal* (101.4 lb. or 46 kilos) is sometimes used.

National Population: 11,797,000 (1984 estimate); population density, 41 per square mile (16 per square kilometer); 83 percent urban and 17 percent rural; annual growth rate, 1.5 percent; age distribution: 0-14 years old, 32.2 percent; 15-59 years old, 59.7 percent; over 60, 8.1 percent

Cities (1980 official estimate):

Santiago	3,899,495
Viña del Mar	277,068
Valparaíso	266,354
Concepción	200,602
Talcahuano	187,507
Antofagasta	162,656
Temuco	157,258
Rancagua	130,940
Talca	129,926
Arica	117,288
Chillán	117,074
Valdivia	110,486

Groups Immigrating at Various Times: Spaniards, Basques, Germans, English, Irish, Swiss, Italians, French, Yugoslavs, and Lebanese.

Ethnic Groupings (estimates vary): Mestizo (of mixed European and Indian ancestry), 66 percent; Spanish, 25 percent; Indian, 5 percent.

GEOGRAPHY

Borders: 3,930 mi. (6,325 km) of land borders
North: Peru
West and South: Pacific Ocean
East: Bolivia and Argentina

Possessions: In the South Pacific, Chile owns Easter Island, Sala y Gómez, San Félix, San Ambrosio, and the Juan Fernández Islands. It also owns the Diego Ramírez Islands southwest of Cape Horn. Chile also claims about 482,500 sq. mi. 1,249,675 km²) of Antarctica lying between 53° W and 90° W. This is the Palmer Peninsula sector. Argentina and Great Britain also claim part of this area.

Sea Rights: Chile claims a limit of 3 nautical mi. for its territorial waters and a limit of 200 nautical mi. for its fishing zone.

Highest Point: Ojos del Salado, 22,539 ft. (6,870 m)

Lowest Point: Sea level

Rivers: About thirty rivers start in the Andes and go to the Pacific, but waterfalls and cascades limit shipping. Chile's longest river is the Loa, in northern Chile, flowing for about 300 mi. (483 km).

Inland Waterways: 451 mi. (725 km)

Mountains: The Andes Mountains run down the eastern side of the country. The range has many volcanoes and snowcapped ridges. In the northern part of Chile, the Cordillera Domeyko (Domeyko mountain chain) runs along the coast parallel to the Andes.

Climate Areas:
Desert north: Extends down to 27° S. Almost rainless; cold water along the coast keeps temperatures down to an average 70° F. (21° C) in summer and 60° F. (16° C) in winter.
Middle Chile: A mild winter and warm, dry summer. Yearly rainfall at Santiago averages 14 in. (35.5 mm). Santiago's average winter temperature is 52° F. (11° C); summer, 69° F. (21° C).
South Chile: South of Bío-Bío River. Despite its latitude, winters are mild. Valdivia temperature averages 46° F. (8° C) in winter and 62° F. (17° C) in summer. In all seasons, heavy rainfall occurs; Valdivia, for example, averages 86 in. (220 cm) yearly.

Lakes: The major lakes of the famous Lake District are lakes Rancho, Villarrica, Puyehue, Todos los Santos (which is really an inlet), and Llanquihue.

Distances:
Maximum width: 236 mi. (380 km)
Narrowest point: 56 mi. (90 km)
Length: 2,650 mi. (4,265 km)

Coastline: 3,999 mi. (6,436 km)

Area: 292,058 sq. mi. (756,430 km²), not including Antaractic claim. Land use estimates: 47 percent barren mountain, desert, and urban; 29 percent forest; 15 percent permanent pasture and meadow; 7 percent other arable; 2 percent cultivated.

NATURE

Animals: Besides the common domestic animals of the Western world, Chile has the llama and alpaca, cousins of the camel. Wild animals include the guanaco, vicuña, fox, deer, penguin, rhea, and the coipo (which looks like a beaver). The condor, one of the largest birds of prey in the world, lives in the Andes. Its body can be more than three feet (91 cm) long, with a wingspread of almost 17 feet (518 cm). There are many whales in Chilean waters and six species of seals.

Chile has several endangered species. One is the pudú, the smallest deer in the world at 15.5 in. (472 cm) tall. Another is the huemul, a native deer that appears on the national coat of arms. The chinchilla, a native rodent, has been hunted indiscriminately in the past for its fur. The black-necked swan, found in central and southern lakes, is protected in national parks and sanctuaries.

Other interesting animals include the puma; three different types of flamingos; and the giant hummingbird, the largest hummingbird in the world.

Coastal Fish: Sardines, bonito, tuna, swordfish, anchovy, corvina, eel, octopus, abalone, lobster, clam

Inland Fish: Salmon, trout

Vegetation:
Atacama Desert: Vast areas support no plant life. Along the coast are some seasonal-flowering herbs and resinous perennials. On the Andes slopes, cactuses and desert shrubs grow.

Central Chile: Stunted palms grow along the coast. In lowlands, blackberry and scrub are common. There are also evergreen forests, Lombardy poplars, eucalyptus, and weeping willow.

South Chile: There is a thick evergreen forest. In the far south, it gives way to grass and heath lands, which are favored by the severe climate.

Native trees include the alerce (larch), araucaria, canelo (cinnamon tree), coigüe, laurel, lingue, mañío, raulí, and roble (oak). Other species include the hazelnut, palm, hawthorn, soapbark, poplar, myrtle, and eucalyptus.

ECONOMY AND INDUSTRY

Gross National Product (total value of goods and services): $20 billion (1980); $1,800 per person. The economy grew in 1980 at a rate of 5 percent.

Principal Products:
Agriculture: Citrus fruit, wheat, oats, corn, onions, rice, barley, rye, beans, peas, potatoes, flax, hemp, and sunflowers are major crops. Sugar beets, grapes, clover, alfalfa, vetch, melons, peppers, and noncitrus fruits also are grown. Livestock include cattle, sheep, pigs, and horses.

Seafood: Sardines, mackerel, hake, anchovies, mussels, clams, and lobsters. (Seafood catch in 1980: 2.8 million metric tons; exports, $339 million in 1979.)

Mining and other extracting: Copper is Chile's most important export (1,240,000 metric tons in 1982). Together with iron and nitrate, it accounts for three fourths of Chile's exports. Chile also produces coal, manganese, lead, zinc, gold, silver, kaolin, molybdenum, iron, mercury, limestone, quartz, slate, pozzuolana, talc, and coal. In 1982, Chile produced 2,484,212 cubic meters of crude oil and 2,505,000 cubic meters of natural gas.

Manufacturing: Steel (765,000 million metric tons capacity in 1980), cement, textiles, clothing, shoes and other leather goods, plastic products, glass, locomotives, radios, refrigerators, hardware, motor vehicles, tires, drugs, soaps, chemicals, pulp and paper, canned vegetables, condensed and powdered milk, wool, lumber, and fish products

Tourism: In 1981, Chile received more than 350,000 foreign tourists.

Labor Force: Approximately 3,340,000 full-time workers in 1980, between 25 percent and 33 percent of the labor force was in labor unions. The largest labor organization, Central Unica de Trabajadores de Chile (CUTCH), was banned by the government in 1973.

Communication: Chile has 152 AM, 81 FM, and 58 TV stations. In 1979, there were 1,200,000 television sets and 3,200,000 radios in use (70,000 television sets and 29,000 radios were manufactured in 1978). Santiago has 29 radio stations. A national TV network and local stations serve various areas. Most broadcasts are black and white. You can make telephone calls to all areas of Chile. In 1980, 554,000 telephones were in use.

Publishing: Journalists publish several hundred newspapers. The oldest is *El Mercurio,* published in Santiago. There are many trade and news magazines. The comic book industry is very busy.

Transportation:
Air: Twenty international airlines serve Chile, including Chile's own privately owned airline. Air traffic within the country is also carried by LADECO as well as by the state-owned Linea Aerea Nacional and smaller carriers. Chile has 341 usable airfields, 44 with permanent-surface runways, 13 with runways over 8,005 ft. (2,440 m) long.
Land: The Chilean section of the Pan-American Highway runs 2,100 miles (3,500 km) from Arica to Chiloé. Inter-American Highway runs north-south from Arica to Llay-Llay. From there, one branch goes on to Santiago. Another crosses the Andes and goes on to Argentina. Another major highway connects Osorno to Argentina via the Puyehue Pass across the mountains. Chile had about 730,000 automobiles, 18,600 taxis and buses, 175,000 trucks, and 17,000 tractors in use at the end of 1981. There are 5,135 mi. (8,293 km) of railroad (using tracks of several widths). One line crosses the Andes at 14,760 ft. (4,500 m). The Metro in Santiago was inaugurated in 1975; its most traveled route connects Santiago with the ports of Valparaíso and San Antonio. There are approximately 34,798 mi. (55,990 km) of roads, of which 5,819 mi. (9,365 km) are paved.
Sea: Chile's merchant fleet has almost 60 vessels of over 100 tons.
Pipelines: Crude oil, 469 mi. (755 km); refined products, 488 mi. (785 km); natural gas, 199 mi. (320 km)

EVERYDAY LIFE

Food: Chileans generally eat their main meal early in the afternoon. They eat supper between 9:00 P.M. and 11:00 P.M. Most schoolchildren come home for lunch, which is followed by a period of rest, called a siesta. Typical dishes include *empanadas* (meat-filled pies), *cazuela de ave* (chicken soup), and *curanto* (fish and meat stew). French cooking is popular with the wealthy. The well-to-do and the middle class often eat seafood such as tuna, swordfish, eel, and shrimp. The most important foods of workers are beans and bread. At meals, Chileans generally drink wine.

Housing: Tenant farmers on big estates generally live in one-room adobe houses. The large homes of the owners are usually Spanish style. The government and several mining companies have provided modern housing for some workers. An estimated 20 percent of Chileans live in shantytowns; some live in tenements. Older-style houses may have 12-foot-high ceilings and foot-thick walls. Houses for rent or sale are scarce, so most people live in apartments. Earthquakes occur, so few buildings are over 10 stories tall.

Public Holidays:
January 1, New Year's Day
Two days during Holy Week
May 1, Labor Day
May 21, Navy Day
August 15, Assumption of the Virgin
September 18, National Independence Day

September 19, Armed Forces Day
October 12, Columbus Day
November 1, All Saints' Day
December 8, Immaculate Conception
December 25, Christmas

Seasonal Events: Ballet, theater, and opera season: April to November; International Song Festival at Viña del Mar: February; Flower shows: around October and November; Farming and industrial exhibitions in Santiago: October.

Culture: Since subjugation of the Inca and of the Araucanian Indians by the Spaniards, Spanish culture has held sway. The National, Congressional, and university libraries have large collections of books, ranging from Spanish classics to those of other countries. There are many *museos* in Chile, a name that also applies to art galleries. They vary from displays of Indian artifacts in such towns as San Pedro de Atacama to an aircraft museum in Santiago. Santiago also has the Museum of Natural Science, the National Museum, the Museum of History, and the Palace of Fine Arts. It also has two observatories and about twelve legitimate theaters. The universities actively promote theatrical performances. Chilean poets and musicians are highly respected internationally. Santiago has two symphony orchestras. The United States supplies most of Chile's movies.

Education: The minister of education controls schools. In 1978, 71 percent of those aged 5 to 19 were in school. About 30 percent of students attend private schools, which are government approved. The law requires school attendance of children from 7 to 15 years of age, but it is poorly enforced. Classes run from March through December. Preschool children may attend nursery or kindergarten programs until they are 5 years old. Students attend elementary school for eight years. High school emphasizes either arts and science (college preparatory courses) or industrial, technical, commercial, or agricultural courses. There are eight universities (three in Santiago, two in Valparaíso, and Antofagasta, Concepción, and Valdivia each have one). Since the 1973 military takeover, the junta has attempted to rid education of leftist political influences. Military appointees replaced heads of universities. In 1978, about 90 percent of Chileans could read and write.

Social Welfare: Chileans tend to be be very hearty, to enjoy the outdoors, and to be very active. By 1980, the infant mortality rate had declined to 33 per thousand live births. The life expectancy is about 64 years for males, 70 years for females. Government-controlled organizations provide extensive benefits for housing, sickness, maternity, and old-age and unemployment insurance. The largest organization even manufactures low-cost clothing and drugs and runs inexpensive restaurants.

Sports: The most popular sport is *futbol* (soccer). Other popular sports include swimming, field hockey, basketball, gymnastics, boxing, volleyball, golf, tennis, horse racing, hunting, fishing, and skiing.

INDIAN LIFE

Food: Few of the Chilean Indians settled long enough to farm, although those who did raised potatoes, corn, and other vegetables. Most were nomads who traveled while hunting. With slings, arrows, and spears, they would kill ducks, geese, guanaco, deer, and other animals. They were good fishermen.

Houses: Indians who settled along the rivers and in the northern regions often made small homes out of mud, which dried in the sun. Stone walls surrounded clusters of these primitive houses for protection. Other Indians lived in huts made of twigs. Some simply erected windbreakers of skins.

Clothes: Some of the tribes made excellent jewelry, which they wore during feasts. Often their clothing was decorated with shells or silver buttons. The women would wear long capes and skirts that encircled their bodies. The men wore ponchos. Sometimes the warriors decorated their hair with feathers, and they shaved their heads before battle. More remote Indians dressed in clothes made from flattened bark.

Way of Life: The Indians, especially the Mapuche, were very warlike and were not conquered for several hundred years after the Spaniards arrived. Even the well-organized Inca from Peru had a difficult time dealing with the Chilean Indians. However, the Indians eventually were beaten back and placed on reservations when the Chilean frontier opened up in the 1800s. They believed that a world of spirits surrounded them and they were careful not to make the spirits angry. The shaman (priest) was as important as the earring-wearing chief.

IMPORTANT DATES

10,000 B.C. — Indians may have reached Chile

1471 — Inca armies invade what is now Chile

1520 — Ferdinand Magellan sails through strait now named for him

1535 — Spanish expedition under Diego de Almagro attempts conquest of Chile

1540 — Spaniards under Pedro de Valdivia begin conquest of Chile

1541 — De Valdivia founds Santiago

1553 — De Valdivia defeated by Araucanian chief Tucapel and executed

1556 — Garcia Hurtado de Mendoza made captain general of Chile

1557 — Tucapel, Araucanian chief, killed

1558 — National cathedral built

1578 — Valparaíso captured by Sir Francis Drake

1590 — Alonso de Ecrilla y Zúñiga finishes epic poem *La Araucana*

1598-1602 — Indians destroy most of Spanish settlements

1606 — By Spanish royal decree, all Mapuche prisoners of war are to be made slaves

1618 — Church of San Francisco completed in Santiago

1641 — First peace treaty with Mapuche

1674 — Decree withdrawn that enslaved Mapuche war captives

1771 — Church of Santo Domingo inaugurated in Santiago

1778 — Chile elevated to captaincy general; Bernardo O'Higgins born

1802 — O'Higgins returns to Chile after studying in Europe

1810 — Chilean independence proclaimed

1811 — Some slaves freed

1814 — Spain reestablishes control of Chile

1817 — O'Higgins and José de San Martín invade Chile and defeat Spaniards

1817-1823—Bernardo O'Higgins has dictatorial powers

1818—Independence regained

1820-1823—Troops from Chile help to liberate Peru from Spaniards

1822—Valparaíso destroyed by earthquake

1823—Remaining slaves freed; O'Higgins steps down from office and goes to Peru

1825—Mining of nitrate begins in what was then part of Bolivia and Peru (now in Chile)

1826—Fort of San Antonio on the southern island of Chiloé is captured from the Spaniards

1833—New constitution adopted

1835—Massive earthquakes shake Chile

1839—Chile defeats Bolivia and Peru

1842—National University of Chile founded

1843—Penal colony started at what becomes Punta Arenas; Strait of Magellan claimed by Chile

1848—Failed revolution in Germany spurs emigration to Chile

1852—Railroad completed from Caldera to Copiapó; Germans arrive in Chile

1861—After 30 years in power, Conservatives are defeated by Liberals, who then remain in power for the next 30 years

1866—Spaniards attempt to regain control of Chile; they bombard Valparaíso but Chilean navy drives them off

1879-1883—War of the Pacific; Chile defeats Bolivia and Peru and gains mineral wealth in northern desert

1881—Final Araucanian Indian uprising

1883—Indians are restricted to reservations

1888—Chile takes control of Easter Island; Catholic University founded

1891—Civil war after which the congress controls the government for 30 years

1902—Argentina and Chile conclude a border agreement

1904—The statue "Christ of the Andes" is erected above Uspallata Pass to commemorate the 1902 border settlement

1906—Earthquake destroys Valparaíso

1913—Bethlehem Steel Company leases the chief deposits of high-grade iron ore at El Tofo in the province of Coquimbo

1919—University founded at Concepción

1924—Army and navy force President Arturo Alessandri Palma's resignation

1925—New constitution; church and state are separated

1929—Chile cedes province of Tacna to Peru

1931-1932—Economic depression hits Chile; civil unrest; Technical University is established

1939—Earthquake destroys Chillán; government establishes a national development organization (CORFO)

1939-1945—Chile remains neutral during World War II

1945—Gabriela Mistral receives Nobel Prize in literature

1948—Military revolt led by Carlos Ibáñez is suppressed; Chile claims part of Antarctica; Communist party is outlawed

1949—Women gain right to vote

1958—Communist party legalized

1960—Earthquake and tidal wave devastate Corral

1961—Catholic church donates 50,000 acres to the landless

1962—Chile hosts World Cup soccer championships; crisis with Bolivia over Chile's diversion of water from the Lauca River for irrigation

1967—Copper industry is "Chileanized"

1969—Voting age lowered to eighteen

1970—Marxist president, Salvador Allende, elected

1971—Pablo Neruda wins Nobel Prize in literature

1973—Allende's government overthrown by armed forces

1978—Government starts program to train peasants who had been given land

1977—All political parties banned

1981—Pinochet becomes president; new constitution comes into effect; it continues junta's rule to 1989, with phased return to full civilian rule by 1997; huge hydroelectric project starts at Colbun-Machicura-Chiburgo

1983—Low prices for copper and worldwide recession lead to 30 percent unemployment; demonstrations against continuing military rule

1984—Demonstrations continue against military rule

1985—Earthquake measuring 7.4 on the Richter Scale hits central Chile. Thousands of buildings destroyed and hundreds of people killed in Santiago, Valparaíso, and Viña del Mar.

IMPORTANT PEOPLE

Diego de Almagro (1475-1538), Spanish soldier attempted conquest of Chile in 1535

Claudio Arrau (1903-   ), concert pianist

Miguel Luis Amunátegui (1828-1888), historian

Nemesio Atúnez (1918-   ), painter

Edwardo Barrios (1884-1963), novelist

Diego Barros Arana (1830-1907), historian

Gustavo Becerra (1925-   ), teacher and composer

Andres Bello (1780?-1865), scholar and writer; edited civil code of Chile

Arturo Blest Gana (1830-1920), realistic novelist

María Luisa Bombal (1910-   ), short-story writer

Cardinal José Caro (1866-1958), archbishop of Santiago

Thomas Cochrane (1775-1860), helped form Chile's navy

Marta Colvin (1917-   ), sculptor

José Donoso (1925-   ), novelist, short-story writer

Ricardo Donoso (1896-   ), historian

Joaquín Edwards Bello (1888-1968), novelist; newspaperman

Alonso de Ercilla y Zúñiga (1533-1594), soldier and writer of epic poem *La Araucana*

Crescente Errázuriz (1839-1931), archbishop of Santiago

Luis Galdames (1881-1943), historian

Lily Garafulic (1914-   ), sculptor

Luis Alberto Heiremans (1928-1965), playwright

Vicente Huidobro (1893-1948), poet

García Hurtado de Mendoza (1535-1609), governor, consolidates Spanish conquest

José Lastarria (1817-1888), writer and a leader of Chile's first literary movement

Lautaro (1535?-1557), Araucanian Indian chieftain

Baldomero Lilo (1867-1923), realistic short-story writer

Pedro Lira (1845-1902), naturalist painter

Roberto Matta (1912-   ), painter

Gabriela Mistral (1889-1957), poet, won Nobel Prize, 1945

Pablo Neruda (1904-1973), poet, won Nobel Prize, 1971

Bernardo O'Higgins (1778-1842), led fight for independence and was first head of state

Nicanor Parra (1914-   ), poet

Diego Portales (1793-1837), conservative politician, influenced constitution of 1833

Pedro Prado (1886-1952), poetic novelist

Arturo Prat (1848-1879), naval hero in War of the Pacific

Luis Recabarren Serrano (1876-1924), helped organize Workers' Federation of Chile and Socialist Workers' Party

Manuel Robles (1837-1870), composer, wrote Chile's first national anthem

Manuel Rojas (1896-1973), novelist and short-story writer

José de San Martín (1778-1850), Argentinian soldier; helped Chile gain independence

Domingo Santa Cruz (1899-   ), composer and administrator

Silvia Soublette de Valdes (1923-   ), distinguished conductor, singer, and composer

Benjamín Subercascaux (1902-1973), novelist and popular historian

José Toribio Medina (1852-1930), historian

Arturo Torres-Ríoseco (1897-   ), literary critic

Armando Uribe Arce (1933-   ), poet and diplomat

Benjamín Vicuña Mackenna (1831-1886), historian

Pedro de Valdivia (1500-1554), invaded Chile and established Santiago, Concepción, and Valdivia

Ramón Vinay (1912-   ), operatic tenor

PRESIDENTS OF CHILE

Joaquín Prieto	1831-1841	Carlos Ibáñez del Campo	1927-1931
Manuel Bulnes	1841-1851	Short-lived presidencies	1931-1932
Manuel Montt	1851-1861	Arturo Alessandri Palma	1932-1938
José Joaquín Perez	1861-1871	Pedro Aguirre Cerda	1938-1941
Frederico Errázuriz	1871-1876	Juan Antonio Ríos	1942-1946
Aníbal Pinto	1876-1881	Gabriel González Videla	1946-1952
Domingo Santa María	1881-1886	Carlos Ibáñez del Campo	1952-1958
José Manuel Balmaceda	1886-1891	Jorge Alessandri Rodríguez	1958-1964
Congressional rule	1891-1920	Eduardo Frei Montalva	1964-1970
Arturo Alessandri Palma	1920-1924	Salvador Allende Gossens	1970-1973
Arturo Alessandri Palma (interim, 1925)		Military junta	1973-1981
Emiliano Figueroa	1925-1927	Augusto Pinochet Ugarte	1981-

Guanaco (above) are similar
to the domesticated llama,
but run wild. The copihue (left),
Chile's national flower,
is a member of the rose family.

INDEX

Page numbers that appear in boldface type indicate illustrations

For help in preparing the manuscript for *Enchantment of the World: Chile,* the author would like to thank Denis Lustig and Ruth Bandera of Lan Chile Airlines; Mario Correa, cultural attache, and his staff of the Embassy of Chile; the Chilean Development Corporation; Michael Fleet, professor of political science, Marquette University; Charles Paul May; Allan Carpenter; Max Seligman; Jeanne Westphal; Luis Hernan Videla Pacheco of the Automóvil Club de Chile; Gustavo Gutiérrez Aristegui, of Centro de Estudios Turisticos; Jaime Nef Leighton; George E. Saade, Ernesto Byrne, and Arturo Salgado of the Sheraton San Cristobal; Gen. Sergio Piñeiro, commander of Región X; Miguel Veyl, editor of El Llanquihue; Carlos Spoerer; Ana María Soto; and Juan Pazos Fontella and Ester Oyarzo, who make the best curanto in Puerto Montt. Then there are the many, many other Chileans—too numerous to name individually—who have demonstrated their love of country by being warm, friendly, and inviting to guests.

About the Author

Martin Hintz, author of *Chile,* is a journalist based in Milwaukee, Wisconsin. He covered the 1981 inaguration of Chilean President Augusto Pinochet for several news outlets in the United States. Hintz specializes in travel reporting and is a member of the Society of American Travel Writers and the Midwest Travel Writers Association. He and his wife, Sandy, the communications director for the Sacred Heart Fathers and Brothers religious community, have three children: Dan, Steve, and Kate. The family often travels together, researching books and stories for numerous publications. Hintz has a master's degree in journalism from Northwestern University and is a former newspaper reporter.